S0-EKL-806

NEWFIE JOKE BOOK

WARNING: Even if you are not easily offended, you will probably hate yourself for laughing at these jokes!

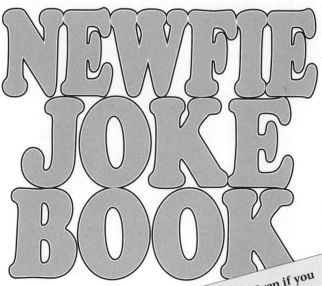

NEWFIE JOKE BOOK

WARNING: Even if you are not easily offended, you will probably hate yourself for laughing at these jokes!

compiled by
Natasha White

FOLK
LORE
PUBLISHING

© 2010 by Folklore Publishing
First printed in 2010 10 9 8 7 6 5 4 3 2 1
Printed in Canada

All rights reserved. No part of this work covered by the copyrights hereon may
be reproduced or used in any form or by any means—graphic, electronic
or mechanical—without the prior written permission of the publisher,
except for reviewers, who may quote brief passages. Any request for photo-
copying, recording, taping or storage on information retrieval systems of
any part of this work shall be directed in writing to the publisher.

The Publisher: Folklore Publishing
Website: www.folklorepublishing.com

Library and Archives Canada Cataloguing in Publication

White, Natasha, 1974–
Newfie joke book / Natasha White.

Includes bibliographical references.
ISBN 978-1-926677-39-2
    1. Canadian wit and humor (English)—Newfoundland and Labrador.
2 Newfoundland and Labrador—Humor. I. Title.

PN6178.C3W54 2010   C818'.602   C2010-900065-X

Project Director: Faye Boer
Project Editor: Carla MacKay
Cover Image: Roger Garcia
Back Cover Image: Photos.com
Illustrations: Roger Garcia

We acknowledge the support of the Alberta Foundation for the Arts for
our publishing program.

We acknowledge the financial support of the Government of Canada
through the Book Publishing Industry Development Program (BPIDP) for
our publishing activities.

 Canadian   Patrimoine
Heritage   canadien

Contents

Dedication

To my parents. Thank you for your words of
encouragement, your down-home advice and for
being sensible enough to stay on The Rock.

Introduction

Whatta ya at me, son? (Or, how are you doing?) It seems fairly obvious at this point that you have bought or been given a book on Newfie humour. With the printing of this book, it's also probable that someone, somewhere, is going to start the debate—again—about the derogatory nature of Newfie jokes. It's likely this argument has been around as long as the jokes themselves, and I am quite sure I won't be putting an end to things in these pages.

I consider myself a Newfie. I was born and raised around the bay—Dildo, to be exact. I left home to discover what the rest of Canada had to offer, and, let me tell you, life on the mainland, when your parents' address is back in Dildo, has not always been the laughing matter you might think.

My personal opinion on the Newfie versus Newfoundlander debate is this: I know "Newfoundlander" is the correct term for someone who resides on the island of Newfoundland, but I believe "Newfie" is a term that we born-and-breds wear with pride when we are talking about our ability to laugh at ourselves in the face of the rest of Canada's seemingly unyielding criticism. I have faced that criticism as a Newfoundlander and come out on the other side as a Newfie. I left home ashamed to say where I was from, but now I am proud to tell anyone that yes, I am from Dildo.

Newfie jokes are told from coast to coast, by Newfoundlanders and mainlanders alike.

The jokes are told to get a laugh or to put us down. They arcn't always true and they aren't always funny, but you can rest assured that they will break the ice—just take care to gauge the thickness of that ice before you start telling the jokes. When you recite a joke about a distinct group of people, remember that funny can quickly turn into derogatory, and sometimes the line between these two is so fine that it's easy to cross and not realize what you have done until it's too late.

I, however, can tell the jokes in this book, secure in the knowledge that some of them are true and some of them represent the truth as I see it. While I may not be personally acquainted someone who has done all of the joke-worthy things in this book, I see small bits of what I know in almost every story. Most people would be surprised at the Newfie stories and jokes that are fact and not attempts at humour...

Newfie or Newfoundlander, take the time to read these stories and jokes, and look for the truth and humour behind each one. Each of us has an aunt or grandparent who has done something comical. We all know the person down the lane who has never left the community and is oblivious to the world outside their home. And, lastly, for those of us who have moved away from The Rock, we have all stood in the middle of a big city and shown, whether we meant to or not, that we were small-town dwellers at heart.

❧❋❧

CHAPTER ONE

Newfanese

> *We Newfies are famous for the way we speak. While our dialects stem from years of isolation, our slang often owes its roots to England and Ireland, with some throwbacks to Scotland and France, and even the most sophisticated Canadian will tell you they can recognize a Newfie just by the way he or she talks. We have our own dictionary. We have our own speech patterns that seem unintelligible to everyone else. We can talk so fast that no one else understands us. And we like it that way.*

To be honest, I think Newfie jokes are meant to be told aloud. When you read a Newfie joke, you hear none of the accent or inflection. The injustice! However, when you tell a Newfie joke, you have the opportunity to infuse it with your own interpretation of the language. But how can you learn to utter this delicate language that permeates the island's tongues? And how can you recite your Newfie jokes with the best effect? With this simple three-step process, that's how:

Step 1: Learn the base language.

Step 2: Study the accent.

Step 3: Master the slang of the island.

Step 1: Learn the Base Language

Many people will disagree that Newfanese is based on English. As the many naysayers will tell you, Newfanese sounds like a completely different language. Let me be the one to dispel the myth. Newfanese is, indeed, an offshoot of English. It (loosely) shares its grammar and sentence structure with proper English, and it also uses nouns, pronouns, verbs and sentences—who cares if they are used in ways that make people shake their heads? But, there are a few places in which Newfanese differs greatly from English, and those areas are subject and verb agreements, pronouns and adjectives.

Subject and Verb Agreements

Forget the idea that verbs and subjects of sentences need to agree. Newfies have long forgone the strict grammar rule that says if the subject of your sentence is singular then the verb of the sentence must be singular, too. Let's look at an example. Stay calm if you don't understand all the slang; we'll get to that in Step 3.

Newfanese

Gets me that, chummy—Get me that, chummy.

You is on the other side—You are on the other side.

I takes a look at my wife—I take a look at my wife.

Where the hell is we?—Where the hell are we?

You knows you're my one true love—You know you're my one true love.

See what I'm talking about? Simple Newfanese grammar rule of thumb: if you is talking about a bunch of stuff, make the verb for one, and if you is talking about one thing, make the verb for a bunch of stuff (i.e. make singular verbs plural and plural verbs singular). But wait! This rule doesn't apply to every sentence. You have to pick and choose the best ones to mess up. How silly would you sound if you applied the rule to a whole paragraph? You would sound as foolish as odd socks, for sure. Apply the rule sparingly, for effect. You don't want to appear as though you grew up around the bay, you just wants to look like you visited there for a while.

Pronouns

Pronouns are a closely guarded secret on the island of Newfoundland. To make sure they are distinct from the rest of Canada, Newfies have invented their own set of pronouns to replace the previously long-standing ones used in proper English. English-speaking Canadians use "him" and "her," but Newfies prefer using "buddy" and "missus." If you need to say, "That's his fishing boat," you can replace "his" with "buddy" and end up with "That's buddy's fishing boat." Everyone in Newfoundland will know you mean "his," even if they don't have a clue who "buddy" is.

Adjectives

Newfies also have a special way of using positive and negative adjectives. For instance, a negative adjective can be used in a positive way and positive adjective can be used in a negative way, and sometimes Newfies just ignore the meaning of the adjective altogether and use it to describe size. Two of the most commonly used Newfie adjectives are "awful" and "wonderful."

Newfanese

That was some awful nice present you gave me—Thank you for the really great present.

That was some wonderful big storm—That storm was really powerful.

That was awful nice of you—You were really nice to me.

That pain was wonderful bad—The pain was really horrible.

Step 2: Study the Accent

Step 1 finished. Now for Step 2. Newfie accents are one of the hardest things in Newfanese to nail down. At times, they can be as slippery as tomcods. The issue is that there are many different accents in

Newfoundland, and if you know the accents, you can tell where someone is from just by listening to them speak. For example, if someone lives on the Southern Shore, they are more likely to sound like they are from Ireland. But if someone is from Notre Dame Bay, they might drop the leading *h* from a word and add it onto another random word that starts with a vowel. And if someone is from the Northern Peninsula...well, they have been so far away from everyone and everything for so long, we all have problems understanding them. Let's just say they talk really, really fast.

To help you learn a general Newfie accent, it's best to focus on just a few simple lessons: change the way you speak, drop a few *h*'s, lose a whole pile of *g*'s and remove *th* from your vocabulary.

Change the Way You Speak

This might be the hardest part to learn. It requires that you forget how you usually say simple words like "park" and "car," and instead pronounce them differently. When most Canadians say "park," it sounds like "poark" to Newfies. We stick with the classic "park" (making the *ar* sound as if we're saying "are"). Perhaps that's our pirate connection sneaking into the 21st century. Anyway, use that same pronunciation with words like "garage," another good example. Newfies hear Canadians say "ga-rage" (all the syllables are lengthened), but Newfies say "g'rage" (we shorten the syllables—think "grrage").

Newfies are also famous for running their syllables together, shortening a word so they can say it faster. For example, Canadians say "at all" (two syllables, the word "at" and the word "all"), while Newfies speed up the whole process and the word comes out sounding like "a'toll."

Newfanese

Landri—Laundry

Bax—Box

S'pose—Suppose

'Nuff—Enough

So basically, just make your words sound harsh (think of guttural German sounds) and say them really quickly. Trust me, Newfies will know exactly what you're saying if you pronounce "better" as "betr."

Drop a Few H's

Dropping and adding *h*'s is one of the more telltale signs of a Newfie accent. The greatest concentration of *h*-droppers might be around Notre Dame Bay, but the practice is definitely not limited to that part of the island. When dropping *h*'s the rule is simple: pronounce the word like it has no *h*. For example, "high" is pronounced "'igh" or "height" is pronounced "'eight." The *h*-dropping phenomenon is closely paired to the idea of adding *h*'s to words that start with a vowel. For example, in Newfoundland the word "eye" is pronounced "heye" (think high) and the word "eight" is pronounced "height" (think hate). As our tried-and-true saying goes, "I lost my *H* in 'olyrood and found it again in Havondale." (Holyrood and Avondale are towns in Newfoundland.)

The dropping and adding of *h*'s can be confusing for the uninitiated. The words have to be understood in context; I mean, you have *know* what the Newfies are talking about so you can understand what the Newfies are talking about! Take, for instance, this miscommunication between a young child learning her spelling and the father who is quizzing her.

He says, "Spell ''igh.'"

She says, "E-Y-E."

He says, "No, spell ''igh.'"

She says, "Capital *I*."

He says, "Now come on, you knows you can spell ''igh.'"

She says, "Well, let me see the word." He shows her "high."

She says, "Oh, you mean spell 'high.'"

He says, "Right, I says spell ''igh.'"

Don't get confused. Most of the time there will be a secret word that gives away the context of *h*-dropping or -adding that allows you to understand what is being said. Look for the hint, and you should be fine.

Newfanese

'Igh school—High school

Heye surgery—Eye surgery

Hairport—Airport

Secret Word

School (you know the only type of school with any word close to "'igh" in it is high school).

Surgery (the only part of the body that can be operated on that has something to do with "heye" is the eye).

Port (the only common mode of transportation "port" has anything to do with is air—unless you're talking about a barber shop that likes to use a play on words in its name).

See? It all seems obvious now, doesn't it?

Lose a Whole Pile of G's:

Now, it seems that if a group of people drop and add *h*'s to the beginnings of their words, it would also seem logical if they had a rule about dropping *g*'s, they would drop them at the beginning of their words as well—not so for Newfies. *G*-dropping is a favourite accent twist found almost all over the island, but it only applies to words that end in *g*. You can't go around dropping the leading *g* from words like "good," "garage" or "God" (Newfies do not say "'ood," "'arage" or "'od"). Instead, *g*'s get dropped from the ends of words that end in *ing*—gerunds, for those in the know. Newfies say their word quickly and drop the *g*. This habit can be applied to almost any word ending in *ing*.

Newfanese

Anythin'—Anything

Goin'—Going

Nothin'—Nothing

Remove th *From Your Vocabulary*

Dropping and adding *h*'s applies to the beginnings of words and dropping *g*'s applies to ends of words, but in strict Newfanese *th* gets the chop, too. In the case of *th*, though, it can be removed from the middle of a word, it can be changed to a *t* sound or it can be made into a *d* sound. Strictly speaking, Newfie dialect has been built through many centuries, and the rules are as fluid as bog water (not winter bog water, though, just summer bog water that, when you think about it, isn't fluid at all...).

But that's another story. Back to the *th*'s. Newfies know instinctively how to handle any *th*'s that come their way. It's almost like a jig—no one knows the steps, but everyone knows how to dance. You learn how to transform your *th*'s through careful listening, but there are a few rules you can take to your grave. Leading *th*'s can almost always be replaced by a *d* sound. Thus, "this" is turned into "dis."

Sometimes *th*'s in the middles of words are also dropped, as in the case of "something," which can become "some'in" and, of course, "somethin'." To make things even more clear, *th*'s in the middles of words can be made into a *t* sound—i.e. "anything" becomes "anyt'ing." This *t* transformation can also include the *t* at the end of a word, such as the word "death" pronounced "deat'" (sounds like "debt").

Newfanese

Nuttin' or nuddin'—Nothing

Mout'—Mouth

Teet'—Teeth

Unfortunately, as I'm sure you've noticed by now, Newfanese is not always strictly bound to one rule or another. But it all makes sense. Right? Just remember that if you apply the rules sparingly and with confidence, you'll get the desired effect without looking like you studied for a test.

Step 3: Master the Slang of the Island

Slang abounds in most cultures in the world. Newfies are no different. They enjoy a healthy amount of slang that no one in their right mind can decipher. And just like everywhere else, Newfoundland slang requires that you know what it means before trying to use it effectively. Slang has to be memorized, and if you're really serious about blending in with the Newfies, please take the time to commit to memory the following common slang. It will add depth to your Newfanese and guarantee that you don't look like a come-from-away (CFA).

Newfies have two types of slang: simple slang (that refers to one or a few words) and complex slang (that refers to whole sentences representing a single concept). For the novice Newfanese speaker, start with the simple and work your way up to the complex.

Simple Newfanese

Arse—Ass. Use "arse" when "ass" just won't do.

Bayman—Normally refers to someone who lives around the bay, east of the overpass, just outside of St. John's

Bridge—Landing on the outside of a house, a deck or veranda.

Buddy—Male whose name you don't know, a male whose name you know but you choose not to say or someone whose name is actually Buddy.

B'y—Probably the most famous piece of Newfie slang to leave The Rock. Used to reference someone or something that has to do with the situation, in the same way "eh" is used in Canada.

Chummy/chummyjigger—Object being pointed at or spoken about.

Come-from-away (CFA)—Someone who isn't from Newfoundland. Also typically known as a mainlander.

Contrary—Opposed to an opinion.

Crooked—Cranky or pissed off. You become crooked after you've been contrary.

Dirt—Favourite among mothers who try to steer their children in the right direction. Refers to things you shouldn't do, and has little to do with dirt on the ground. For example, if you go out and have a beer and your mother doesn't approve, she might say to you that drinking beer is "dirt."

Froze—Frozen. Refers to what happens to something in the freezer or to someone who's cold. The word "death" can dramatically increase the power of "froze"—"I nearly froze to death."

Green—A berry (raspberry, blueberry, partridgeberry, etc.) that isn't ripe. "Green" refers to state of ripeness, not colour, of the berry.

Jannying—Wearing a costume to hide your identity. Children go out jannying on Halloween.

Jezly—Irritating to the nth degree. Sometimes "friggin'" just can't express the right emotion.

Jiggs dinner—One-pot meal consisting of salted beef, cabbage, potatoes, carrots, turnip and peas pudding.

Lodge—To set down or place something. If you try to pass someone a plate, and they can't carry anything else, they might tell you to "lodge" it on the counter.

Luh—Replacement for the word "look." If you see a penny on the sidewalk, you can point at it and say "luh," and every Newfie will look.

Maid—Young woman who isn't married.

Machine—Item whose name can't be remembered.

Me dear—Friendly term of endearment ("my dear" can also be used but is generally more of a sharp warning than a term of endearment). You don't have to know the person you call "me dear." It can be used in Tim Hortons and gas stations around the province.

Me son—Anyone who is male and is, generally, younger than the person who's speaking. Can be interchanged with "my son." The difference between the two is where the stress is placed. You say, "*Listen here*, me son," but also say, "*My son*, you listen here" ("me son" is said quickly and "my son" is said slower with the "my" stressed).

Miss—Formal term for an older woman in a position of authority. Includes, but is not limited to, a teacher or a Sunday school teacher.

Missus—Female whose name you don't know or a female whose name you know but don't want to say.

Mummering—Wearing a costume to hide your identity at Christmas. Mummering is an old tradition borrowed from the English.

Nish—Wimpy with a capital *W*. "My God, you're some nish, b'y," means you are a wuss.

Rotted—Really angry at something or some-one. "I'm right rotted at you."

Saucy—To talk back. Usually said by a mother or teacher to a child.

Squish—Not straight. You might say that a painting is "squish" on the wall.

Stunned—Stupid. "B'y, you're as stunned as me arse." (See? "Ass" just wouldn't do.)

Time—A dinner and a dance, usually held in a hall in the community.

Townie—Someone who lives in St. John's. Can be used to refer to someone who lives in Mount Pearl, but townies don't appreciate this.

> **Weather**—Bad weather. "I think we're going to have weather tonight" means you think there's going to be a storm.
>
> **Wha'**—Direct replacement for the word "what." A single-word question typically used when you don't hear what someone else says. "Wha'?"

Going this far, you can see that Newfanese is a colourful language that in some ways reflects English and in other ways throws it right out the window. The following is a list of complex Newfanese that shows just how difficult it can be to understand a language's nuances if you aren't first made privy to their contexts.

Complex Newfanese

A sin—Way to describe an act of meanness committed by you or performed against you.

"Best, kind."—"I'm getting along very well, thank you."

By the each—One thing separate from another. "Can I buy the shirt and pants by the each?"

Dressed up like a stick of gum—In your Sunday best.

Face and eyes into it—Eat really fast or jump right into something.

Get clear of me—Get away from me.

Got more tongue than a logan—Talks a lot. (A logan is a winter boot. It's rubbered around the foot and is leathered around the ankle. It laces up and has a tongue that runs from the middle of the foot to the middle of the shin—in other words, it has a huge tongue.)

"I didn't know whether to shit or go blind."—"I didn't know what to do."

In the slings—Extremely messy; might be used during home renovations.

Keel over—Fall over in disbelief or after having too many drinks.

Like a birch broom in the fits—Messy.

Mug up—Lunch that's made over an open fire in the woods.

"Oh, me nerves!"—Exclamation of irritation.

Scoat his guts out—Work really hard.

Side by each—Side by side.

Steal the eyes right out of your head—Way to describe an untrustworthy person.

As you can see, Newfies really do have their own language. Need more proof…?

Newfanese Bad Weather

'Tis cold 'nuff to skin ya—It's really cold outside.

Some dirty out der, me son—The weather is really bad outside.

Not fit out der—The weather is pretty bad outside.

Cold 'nuff outside to hang meat—It's colder than a fridge outside.

Newfanese "Who Are Your Parents?"

Who made you?—Who are your parents?

Who crocheted you?—Who is your mother?

Who owns you?—Who is your father?

Newfanese Car Parts

Back 'er back—Put it in reverse

Blinker/dinker—Signal light

Bonnet—Hood

Pan—Truck bed

Squat—Dent

Screw up your window—Roll up your window

Newfanese Clothes

Braces—Suspenders

Duster—Housecoat

Farks—The crotch of the pants

Piss pumps—Slippers

Rubbers—Rain boots

Slacks—Dress pants

Step-ins—Underwear

Stocking cap—Toque

T'umb gluttons—Mittens with a thumb and a forefinger

Vamps—Wool socks

Newfanese "I'm Hungry"

I'm starved deat'—I'm starving to death.

I could eat the leg off the lamb of God—I'm hungry!

My throat thinks my stomach's been cut—I haven't had food in such a long time that my stomach thinks it's never getting any more.

I could eat the legs off the table—I'm so hungry I could eat anything, even wooden table legs.

I could eat the arse off a low-flying duck— I'm so hungry that I'm willing to catch something wild to eat.

Looked at me like I was a turkey dinner— They were so hungry they looked at me like I was a delicious turkey dinner.

I could eat the arse off a dead skunk— I'm so hungry that I think it might a good idea to eat a skunk's behind.

I could eat the back door buttered— I'm so hungry I'll eat anything, as long as there's butter on it.

And some Newfanese that needs no English translation...

Newfanese "You're Ugly"

If I had a face like dat, I'd walk backwards.

You've got a face on you like a squid that's been hauled out of the water and jumped on.

You've got a face on you like a bucket of Ski-Doo parts.

She's got a face on her like a half-chewed caramel.

He's got a face like a boiled boot.

You've got a face like a hen's ass.

You've got a face only a mudder could love.

You've got a face only a fadder could love on payday.

She fell out of the ugly tree and hit every stick on the way down.

Newfanese "You're Pretty"

You're some doll, you is.

So cute, I could chew the face right off ya.

There is a lot of Newfanese slang, and these pages cover just the tip of the iceberg. Talking like a Newfie and understanding our slang are the first steps toward enjoying the reading and telling of Newfie jokes. So take a break, practice your *h*'s and disses and dats and in no time a'toll you'll be talkin' like you lives here.

CHAPTER TWO

Hunting, Fishing and Everything Outdoors

Newfies love the outdoors. Well, baymen love the outdoors, and townies love to go around the bay to get to the outdoors. Fishing and hunting, besides being a way of life, are also a bona fide pastime in Newfoundland. Quads and Ski-Doos are common modes of transportation, and no self-respecting bayman would ever admit that he doesn't own either.

A mainlander is driving though central Newfoundland and is completely amazed by the natural beauty he finds all around him. He decides to stop, stretch his legs and go for a walk along the Exploits River. The mainlander follows a path that winds through the woods, but after walking for a while, he doesn't seem to get any closer to the river. It's getting late, but he still wants to see the river, so he leaves the path and follows the sound of rushing water. By the time he gets to the Exploits River, it's dark and he knows he won't be able to find his car without help. Just when the mainlander figures he's going to have to spend the night in the woods, he spies someone on the far side of the river and calls out to him.

"Excuse me, sir, I need help finding my car!" calls the mainlander.

"Wha'?" yells the Newfie.

"I'm lost!" screams the mainlander.

"Wha'?" yells the Newfie. "Come 'ere and tell me what you needs."

"How do I get to the other side?" asks the mainlander.

"Oh. You is already on the other side," replies the Newfie before quickly disappearing into the woods.

Q: Why did the Newfie want to be buried with his quad?

A: Because he never met a hole it couldn't get out of.

Three Newfies are going moose hunting, and their buddy Ed figures out that they have enough supplies to last them a whole week. But about three days into their week of hunting, the b'ys start running out of the essentials. The group sends Ed into Gander with a list of things they need.

Ed comes back with a few bottles of rum, several cases of beer and two packages of hot dogs.

The b'ys look at Ed, then they look at what he bought and say, "My God, Ed, what the hell are we s'posed to do with the hot dogs?"

A Newfie is boasting to a tourist about how many fish he can catch by hand. He tells the tourist that all Newfoundlanders can jig cod faster than a boat can trawl them. The tourist figures that after hearing the Newfie's speech, fishing can't be that hard, after all. The tourist rents all the top-notch gear he can find and sets off on a fishing expedition. He returns from his fishing trip with a 20-pound codfish, and that's it. Quite proud of himself, he stands at the end of the wharf to have his picture taken. The Newfie walks by carrying a string of five tiny rock cods. He takes one look at the tourist, shakes his head and says, "Only caught one, b'y. 'Tis a shame."

A Newfie is coming out of the woods after cutting wood all day. He gets home and sits in his kitchen with his hands over his ears, trying to warm them up.

The Newfie looks at his wife and says, "My God, 'tis some cold out there. Me ears is just about froze off me head; they must be the coldest part of your body. Why couldn't they put the damn things under your arms or somewhere warm like that?"

Phrases Never Uttered by a Newfoundlander Who Likes to Go Trouting

1. This is the biggest trout I have ever caught.
2. Our wives should come trouting with us more often.
3. That bog is too deep for my quad; I might get stuck.
4. I'll mow the lawn; fishing can wait.
5. −15° C is too cold to go ice fishing.
6. These lures are a waste of money.
7. I would never dig up my front yard to find bait.
8. That pond is too far off the highway; I'll find a closer one.
9. My truck can't make it over that hill; I'll have to go home.
10. 5:00 AM is too early to go trouting.

Frank, a Newfie living in Fort McMurray, Alberta, gets a phone call that the food fishery back home is going to be open for one weekend this year. He goes to his boss and asks if he can have the weekend off so he can fly to Newfoundland and jig a few codfish. The boss considers Frank's request and then pounces on an opportunity to do something he has never done in a place he has never been. The boss says, "Yes, you can go, if you promise to take me with you."

So Frank books the tickets and in no time the pair is out jigging fish in the bay. The first day Frank jigs from the right side of the boat and catches all the fish that are allowed between the two men. His boss doesn't catch any fish at all. The second day, Frank moves to the left side of the boat, and his boss is happy. He figures he'll be the lucky one and catch all the fish instead of Frank. But just like the day before, Frank catches all the fish that are allowed, and his boss doesn't get so much as a bite. On their way back to shore, Frank's boss finally asks, "Frank, how do you know which side of the boat to fish on?"

Frank replies, "Oh, dat is easy. When I wake up in the mornin' I takes a look at me wife. If she's lyin' on her right side, I fishes from the right side of the boat. And if she's lyin' on her left side, I fishes from the left side of the boat. Twenty years we been married, and she ain't never failed me yet."

Frank's boss looks at him, completely bewildered. "Frank," he says, "what do you do if she's lying on her back?"

Frank laughs. "My son, if my wife is lyin' on her back when I wakes up, I don't go fishin'!"

Did you hear about the Newfie who lost his left arm in a Ski-Doo accident? He's all right now.

Two b'ys are going fishing and they take along a cooler-full of sandwiches and beer. The pair hike to a pond and set up camp, but Ralphie soon discovers they have forgotten a bottle opener. Jimmy looks at Ralphie and says, "B'y, ya knows you got to go find an opener."

Ralphie shakes his head, "My son, if you t'inks I'm walking away so you can eat all dem sandwiches, you don't know me."

Jimmy says, "My God, Ralphie, what kind of savage do you take me for? I won't eat not one sandwich while you're gone."

Ralphie sets off toward the truck to find an opener. Seven days pass and there is no sign that Ralphie is coming back with the bottle opener, so a near-starving Jimmy reluctantly opens the cooler to fish out a sandwich. All of a sudden, he hears a bloody big roar, and Ralphie jumps out of the bushes. Ralphie yells at Jimmy, "I knew I couldn't trust ya, Jimmy! Now I'm not goin' for that opener for sure."

Two Newfies are living in Fort McMurray, Alberta, and they decide to take a bear-hunting trip. They manage to get a licence and rent an off-road truck for an entire week. After loading up all their gear they drive into the backcountry of northern Alberta. They drive and drive, not really knowing where they are going. At the end of one of the trails, they come upon a sign that reads "Bear Left," so the Newfies turn around and go back to Fort McMurray.

It's a beautiful October day around the bay, and a bayman asks one of his fisherman friends if the winter is going to be cold or mild. The fisherman goes outside, looks to the sky, sniffs the air and announces that the winter will be a cold one. Everyone starts splitting and piling wood, but the fisherman really had nothing to base his decision on so he calls The Weather Network and asks to speak to the weatherman in charge of Newfoundland. The weatherman verifies, indeed, it will be a cold winter.

A week later the warm weather is still holding, and it looks as if it's never going to get cold. The fisherman calls The Weather Network again and asks to speak to the same weatherman. A different man answers the phone, but the fisherman asks if it's going to be a cold winter anyway. The second weatherman tells him that yes, indeed, it looks like it's going to be a cold winter that year.

The fisherman asks, "B'y, how do you fellers figure out the weather? Do you got some fancy equipment up there?"

The weatherman whispers into the phone, "No, sir, but from all accounts, the baymen are cutting wood like mad."

One day, two Newfies are salmon fishing when they see a fisheries officer heading toward them. The Newfies look around, trying to decide what to do. The officer approaches them and without so much as a hello, goodbye or kiss my ass, he demands to see their licences. One of the Newfies drops his rod and goes running though the woods with the fisheries officer chasing after him. Eventually, the Newfie slows to a stop and the officer catches up and says, "Fishing with no licence, eh?"

The Newfie says, "No, b'y," and pulls out a battered salmon fishing licence.

The officer looks confused and asks, "If you have a licence, why did you run?"

The Newfie smiles. "I ran so me buddy could get away. He ain't got a licence."

Murphy's (Quad) Laws

1. The farther away you are from your pickup, the better your chance of getting stuck.

2. If the trail is easy, you're not on the right one.

3. When the weatherman says it will be a sunny day for quading, it won't.

4. The gear you forgot to bring is in your pickup; too bad you aren't.

5. No matter how many quaders you watch drive through a mudhole, you will get stuck.

6. Expensive parts will sacrifice themselves to save cheap parts from destruction.

7. Anything that can go wrong will go wrong at the worst possible moment, at the worst possible location.

8. Downpours usually end when you are driving home in your pickup.

9. After surviving a rough trail, you will get a flat when it gets easy again.

10. Anything you do will cause you to get stuck, even doing nothing.

In Newfoundland, there are two seasons: six months of skidooing and six months of quading.

Garge and Randy are making plans to meet on the wharf at 5:00 AM to go fishing when Garge looks at Randy and says, "B'y, dat's awful early. What if you gets there before me and leaves? How will I know if you was already there and left?"

Randy replies, "Okay den, b'y, here's what we'll do. If I gets der first, I make an *X* on the wharf. And if you gets der first, you can rub it out."

One morning a Newfie in Alberta gets up before the crack of dawn to go ice fishing. He packs up all his gear and heads out to the place his buddies had recently told him about. They said it was the best place they had found yet for ice fishing in Fort McMurray. Half asleep, the Newfie drags his gear, including a friggin' big auger his father sent him for Christmas, out onto the ice.

The Newfie finally gets set up and starts the auger, ready to bore a hole through the ice, when he hears a loud voice say, "There are no fish under the ice."

The Newfie looks around and doesn't see anyone, so he goes back to putting a hole in the ice. Again he hears a loud voice say, "There are no fish under the ice."

The Newfie stops and looks around again, but he can't figure out where the voice is coming from. He lifts his eyes to heaven and whispers, "Is that you, God?" There's no answer, so he shrugs his shoulders and starts back at the hole.

The Newfie then hears the loudest voice yet yell, "I SAID, THERE ARE NO FISH UNDER THE ICE!"

"Jesus Christ, is that you?" the Newfie calls out.

The voice yells back, "No, I'm the manager of the ice rink. Get off the ice now!"

Two Newfies are going camping in Terra Nova National Park. One of them is an educated scientist from St. John's, and the other is his cousin from around the bay who dropped out of school at 15 years old.

The Newfies set up their tent, have a few beers and fall asleep to the sounds of nature. About an hour later, the bayman wakes up the townie and says, "Look up at the sky, tell me what you sees."

The townie replies, "I see about a million stars in the heavens. How quiet and peaceful the world is."

The bayman says to his cousin, "What does that tell you?"

The townie ponders the question and replies, "Well, it tells me that we live in a part of the country where a man can sleep under the stars without fear."

The bayman looks at him strangely and asks, "Seriously, buddy, what does the fact that we are laying in our sleeping bags staring at the stars tell you?"

The townie looks back at his cousin and says, "Cousin dear, I have no idea what you are talking about."

The bayman shakes his head and says, "You ain't as smart as me mudder says. Someone has gone off and stole our tent."

A Newfie living in Ontario finds his joy in fly-fishing. He spends as many weekends as he can standing beside a river, casting his line. One weekend, he wakes up in his tent early on a Sunday morning. It's cold and pouring rain so he decides to head home before he meant to.

When he gets back, it's still dark so he quietly walks into his bedroom, gets undressed and crawls into bed beside his wife without turning on the light. He snuggles up behind her and says, "Some terrible weather out there, darlin'."

His wife responds sleepily, "Yeah, and my stunned-as-a-boot husband is gone fishing all weekend."

Q: Have you heard about the latest anti-theft device in Newfoundland for Bombardier quads?

A: Draping them with Honda or Polaris covers.

Every year, two Newfies go caribou hunting in Labrador, and every year they hire the same company to fly them in. The pilot is different each time, and this year's pilot flies them into the wilderness and drops them off, just as usual. He tells them both, "I'll be back for you in one week. Remember the rule—we can only bring back one caribou."

The pilot returns a week later, and to his surprise the Newfies have shot two caribou. He calls out to the Newfies, "I told you that you can only bring out one caribou!"

One of the Newfies says back, "The pilot last year said the same thing, but we gave him a big tip, and he strapped on the other caribou."

The pilot shakes his head and reluctantly agrees to take the second caribou. The men stow the gear, strap the two caribou to the plane and hop in. The engine strains as it tries to take off. The plane shudders, but the pilot still manages to get the wheels off the makeshift runway. The plane gets about 10 feet in the air, runs out of pavement underneath and slams into the trees. The two Newfies stumble out of the plane, dazed and confused after the crash.

Q: How did the Newfie break his leg while playing hockey with the Toronto Maple Leafs?

A: He fell out of the tree.

One Newfie looks at his friend and says, "Jumpin' dyin', where in the hell are we?"

The other Newfie looks at him and answers, "About 100 feet away from where we crashed last year."

Newfie Hunting Log

MORNING

12:00 AM—Alarm clock rings.

1:00 AM—B'ys come in and drag me out of bed.

1:30 AM—Trow everyt'ing but kitchen sink into pan of truck.

2:00 AM—Leave for da great outdoors.

2:15 AM—Back out of driveway, forgot gun. Go back for gun.

2:30 AM—Drive like idiot to get to woods before daylight.

3:30 AM—Fall asleep at wheel, buddy takes over drivin'.

5:30 AM—Set up camp. Forgot the Jezly tent.

6:00 AM—Head into woods.

7:05 AM—See two moose, a cow and a bull.

7:06 AM—Take aim and squeeze trigger.

7:07 AM—CLICK.

7:08 AM—Load gun as moose walk over closest hill.

8:00 AM—Head back to camp.

9:00 AM—Still is looking for camp.

10:00 AM—Realize got no idea where friggin' camp is.

AFTERNOON

2:00 PM—Fire gun to signal buddies; eat some wild berries.

2:15 PM—Run out of bullets; moose come back.

2:20 PM—Stomach starts to feel little bit off.

2:30 PM—Realize ate poison berries. Start getting sick.

2:45 PM—Rescued.

2:55 PM—Rushed to emergency room to have stomach pumped; throw up all over truck instead.

3:15 PM—Return to camp.

3:30 PM—Leave camp with gun.

4:00 PM—Return to camp for bullets.

4:01 PM—Load gun. Leave camp again.

EVENING

5:00 PM—Empty gun on nipper that won't go away.

6:00 PM—Return to camp. Watch bull graze near truck.

6:01 PM—Load gun.

6:02 PM—Fire gun.

6:03 PM—Bull gets angry, charges the truck.

6:04 PM—Discover dead radiator.

6:05 PM—Buddies return, dragging the cow.

6:06 PM—Get right mad. Almost shoot buddies.

6:07 PM—Get beer from truck. Trip on log. Fall in fire.

6:10 PM—Change clothes. Throw burned ones in fire.

6:15 PM—Take truck, and leave buddies in woods with moose.

6:25 PM—Truck boils over.

6:26 PM—Start walking back to camp.

6:30 PM—Stumble, fall down, drop gun in mud.

6:32 PM—Look up from mud and face angry bull from near the truck.

6:35 PM—Climb tree and yell for buddies to help.

12:00 AM—Get home. Vow never to go hunting again.

Fred and Garge, two baymen living in Ontario, decide they want to go on a fishing trip. Neither one of them has any fishing gear, so they rent everything they need—the rods, the boat, a truck and even a cabin in the woods. Between the two of them they spend a small fortune for a single fishing trip.

The first day they go out and catch nothing. The same thing happens on the second day. On the third day, they still don't catch any fish. This goes on until the last day of their trip, when Fred manages to catch a single trout.

Both men are depressed during their drive back home. Fred looks at Garge and says, "You know what? That there lousy fish cost us more than $5000."

Garge looks at him and replies, "Lordy jumpin' dyin', 'tis a good thing that we didn't catch any more!"

Two Newfies are moose hunting in central Newfoundland. They had been gone almost a week and hadn't even spotted a moose, let alone had a chance to shoot one. On the last day of their trip, they don't bother driving the quad and instead walk into the woods for one last chance to get their moose. They happen upon a lone bull, and one of the Newfies manages to get a shot off and kills the moose where it stands.

The Newfies start hauling the bull out of the woods by the tail. It takes the men hours just to get it to the road, and they still have to pull it more than a kilometre to get to it back to the truck. Another hunter happens to walk by, and he asks them why in God's name they are pulling a moose by the tail. The Newfies shrug their shoulders. The other hunter tells them it will be a lot easier to haul the moose the other way 'round. The Newfies thank the other hunter, walk around to the head of the moose and start dragging it as instructed. About an hour after switching ends, one of the Newfies pipes up and says, "Buddy, I now knows that it's easier to drag this moose by the antlers, but how come we keeps getting farther and farther away from the truck?"

Two baymen are walking through the woods on a hunting trip. One of them grabs his chest and falls to the ground in great pain. His friend uses a cell phone to call the police. He tells the police he needs help; he figures his friend is dead. The police officer instructs him to calm down and that he needs some information before he can know how to handle the situation. The officer asks the bayman to make sure the friend is dead. Before the policeman can continue, the phone goes silent until he hears a single

Q: What's the best blueberry-picking advice a Newfie can give you?

A: Don't pick the red ones; they're green.

gunshot. The bayman picks up the cell phone and says, "Okay, me son, now what?"

A father and son are out fishing in the middle of the cove. While they are rowing the small dory, the boy starts asking his father questions.

He asks, "Fadder, what makes this here boat float?"

His father replies, "I don't rightly know dat, me son."

A little while later, the boy thinks up another question. He asks, "Fadder, what makes the sky blue?"

His father replies, "I don't rightly know dat, me son."

The son looks at his father and asks, "Dad, do you care if I asks you all these questions?"

> Q: Did you hear about the Newfies who went to Africa to hunt elephants?
>
> A: They all ended up in the hospital with hernias from carrying the decoys.

His father replies, "My God, no, son. If you stops asking questions, how will you ever learn anything?"

A group of Newfies goes deer hunting in northern Alberta. After a day of hunting, they return to the cabin, one of the b'ys struggling under the weight of a dead deer.

One of the Newfies asks, "Where's Henry at?"

The Newfie who's carrying the deer says, "He's a couple kilometres back der in the woods. He had some kind of stroke or fit or something."

All the hunting buddies stare at him and say, "You left Henry back in the woods in trouble and carried the deer all the way here?!"

The Newfie looks at them and replies, "Well, I was pretty damn sure that no one was gonna steal Henry."

Way back when you could only order fishing gear from the Eaton's catalogue, an old Newfie fisherman sent a letter to Mr. Eaton himself. It said, "Please send me an engine like you shows on page 256 of the catalogue. If it's any good, I'll send the money right away."

After waiting for the engine for two weeks, the man got a letter in the post that read: "Please send the cheque for the engine. If your cheque is any good, we'll mail the engine."

Two Newfies take a fishing trip in northern Ontario. They rent all the gear they need. On the first day, they manage to catch a 30-pound fish. One of the Newfies tells his friend to mark that spot so they can find it again.

The next day, the two Newfies are walking down to the pier to rent their boat, and the first Newfie asks his friend if he marked the spot so they could find it.

His friend tells him he put a big red *X* on the bottom of the boat.

The first Newfie says, "B'y, you're as stunned as a rock! What if we don't get the same boat as we had yesterday?"

Two Newfie cousins are with their families at a cabin around the bay. One of their mothers says to her son, "Davy, I thought I told you to keep an eye on your cousin. Where is he?"

The boy looks up at his mother and says, "Well, 'tis like this, mudder. If he knows as much as he says he knows, he's canoeing, but if he knows as little as I figures he knows, he's out swimming in the pond."

A large lumber camp in BC has put out an ad for an experienced lumberjack. Soon after, a skinny Newfie shows up and knocks on the head lumberjack's door. The lumberjack takes one look at the slim Newfie, laughs in his face and tells him to leave.

The Newfie straightens his shoulders and says, "Listen here, buddy, I've cut down trees all over the world. At least give me a chance to show you fellers what I can do."

The lumberjack rolls his eyes and says, "Fine, I'll give you a shot. See that giant redwood over there? Cut it down with only your axe."

Five minutes later the Newfie knocks on the lumberjack's door and announces that he's finished chopping down the tree. The lumberjack is amazed and asks the Newfie where he learned to cut trees.

The Newfie replies, "In the Sahara Forest."

"You mean the Sahara Desert," corrects the lumberjack.

The Newfie laughs and replies, "Well, yeah, that's what they calls it now."

A Newfie and an Albertan are walking through the woods near Fort McMurray when a huge bear walks into the clearing about 50 feet ahead of them.

The bear spies the two men and starts lumbering toward them. The Albertan drops his backpack, pulls out a pair of sneakers and starts putting them on.

The Newfie looks at him and says, "What the hell are you doing? We gots to get outta here fast. Sneakers won't help you outrun that there bear."

The Albertan looks up at the Newfie and says, "I don't have to outrun that bear; I just have to outrun you."

A young bayman lad shows up late for Sunday school. Because he is usually on time, the teacher asks if anything is wrong. The little boy says that everything is fine. He's late because he was going to go fishing, but his dad told him he needed to go to church.

The teacher is impressed with the boy's father. She asks if his father explained why it is so important for the boy to go to Sunday school.

The little lad looks up at the teacher and says, "Yes, miss, he did. He told me that he didn't have enough bait for both of us to go fishing today."

Two Newfies, Garge and Harvey, go ice fishing. Harvey is catching fish left, right and centre, while Garge doesn't catch one fish the entire day.

Garge leans over and asks Harvey what his secret is.

Harvey replies, "Mmm mmmmm mm mmmm mmmm mmmmm mmmm."

"What's that?" asks Garge.

Harvey replies, "Mmm mmmmm mm mmmm mmmm mmmmm mmmm."

"Huh?" says Garge. "My son, I can't understand a word you is muttering over there."

Harvey spits something into his hand and says, "You needs to keep your worms warm."

Little Johnny is taking care of his baby sister while his parents are off shopping in town. He decides he wants to go fishing, but, of course, he needs to take his sister if he goes.

When his parents get home later that night, Johnny announces, "Listen here, mudder, I'm never takin' her fishin' wit' me again, you hear?"

His mother says, "Now Johnny, I'm sure that she'll eventually learn to keep quiet and not scare away the fish."

Johnny replies, "It ain't the noise she was makin', mudder. She ate all me bait."

A minivan loaded down with gear and children pulls into one of the remaining campsites at Terra Nova National Park. Four children and their parents hop out of the van and immediately start setting up camp. The boys rush to get firewood while the girls and their mother dutifully set up the camp stove.

A nearby camper speaks to the father. He marvels at the children's display of teamwork.

"Ha!" exclaims the father. "We're from St. John's, and I figured out a system years ago—no one uses the bathroom until our camp is set up and ready to go. It's quite a long drive from town to here."

A woman walks into her kitchen to find her Newfie husband carefully walking around with a fly swatter. She asks him what he's doing.

He replies, "I'm huntin' flies, missus."

"Oh!" she says, "Killin' any?"

He quickly answers, "Yes, I already killed tree males and two females."

"How can you tell them apart?" she asks.

He laughs, "Well now, tree of dem were on a beer can and two of dem were on the phone."

Eleven people are being rescued from a sinking ship. There are nine men from the mainland, one Newfie man and one woman all dangling precariously from a rope tied to the bottom of the rescue helicopter. The rope is only strong enough to carry 10 people, so one of them is going to have to let go. The group is having a tough time deciding on who should lose their spot, and no one is openly volunteering. The woman makes a touching speech about how she'll let go because she is used to giving up everything in her life for a man—she waited her whole life for one at home while he went fishing, hunting and drinking with the boys. As soon as she finishes her speech, the Newfie starts clapping his hands.

A game officer is driving down a rural road in northern Alberta when on the side of the road he spies a Newfie sitting beside a large dead bear.

The game officer looks at the Newfie and says, "That's a pretty big bear you've got there, son."

The Newfie replies proudly, "Yes, sir. This is my first bear-huntin' trip and look what I got. Only took one bullet, too."

"Well," says the officer, "it really is a shame. You shot that bear out of season. I have to give you a $500 fine and take away that bear."

A year later, the Newfie shoots another bear, and he finds himself face-to-face with the same game officer.

The officer looks at the Newfie and says, "That's a beautiful animal you shot, son."

"Yes," replies the Newfie, "and it's bear-hunting season this time. Only took one bullet this time, too."

The game warden asks, "Can I see your licence then?"

"Damn," replies the Newfie, "I ain't got no licence, sir."

Q: Where do you find trees in Newfoundland?

A: Always between two and four.

The game officer says, "That's gonna cost you $500, and I'm taking the bear again."

One year later, the Newfie shoots another bear and ends up face-to-face with the same officer once more. The officer says, "You sure are lucky, son.

That's another big bear that you shot. It might be the biggest bear I've seen this year."

"Yup," says the Newfie, "and this year it's hunting season and I got me licence right here, sir."

"Everything seems to be legal," says the officer. "Tell me, son, how many times did you shoot that bear to bring him down?"

"Only once. That's three years in a row, by my count," says the Newfie.

The warden looks at the bear and asks, "Then why does he have a hole in each paw and one in his forehead?"

"Well," says the Newfie, "when I shined the flashlight in his face, he covered his eyes."

Hiker Comments at Gros Morne National Park

Please stop making trails that go uphill.

Too many nippers and flies. Please spray before the next time we arrive.

The places where trails do not exist are not marked well.

Something came into my camp last night and stole my beer. Can I get my money back?

A Newfie leaves work on a Friday afternoon. But instead of going home, he stays out the entire weekend hunting with the b'ys. He also manages to spend his entire paycheque on beer. On Sunday night, when he finally appears at home, he is confronted by his angry wife and nagged for nearly two hours about what he's been doing all weekend. His wife finally stops and yells, "How would you like it if you didn't see me for two or three days?"

The Newfie replies, "By God, that sounds mighty fine to me, missus."

Monday goes by and he doesn't see his wife. Tuesday and Wednesday come and go with the same results. By Thursday, the swelling has gone down just enough to where he can see her a little out of the corner of his left eye.

One summer evening during a violent thunderstorm a mother is tucking her small boy into bed. She is about to turn off the light when he asks with a tremor in his voice, "Mudder, will you sleep in here with me tonight?"

The mother smiles and gives him a big hug. "I can't, dear," she says. "I have to sleep in Daddy's room."

A long silence is broken at last by the boy's shaking little voice, "My God, fadder's some nish."

A fellow stops at an outport gas station in Newfoundland and, after filling his tank, pays the bill and buys a pop. As he stands by his car to drink his Coke, he watches two men working along the road. One man would dig a hole two or three feet deep and then move on. The other man then came along behind and filled in the hole. The men work right past the fellow with the pop and go on down the road.

"I can't stand this," says the man. Tossing the can in a trash, he heads down the road toward the men. "Hold it, hold it," he says. "Can you tell me what's going on here with this digging?"

"Well, 'tis like this, buddy. We works for the government," one of the men says.

"But one of you is digging a hole and the other fills it up. You're not accomplishing anything. Aren't you wasting money?" the man from the gas station asks.

"You don't understand nuthin', buddy," one of the men says, leaning on his shovel and wiping his brow. "Normally there's tree of us...me, Fred and Mikey. I digs the 'ole, Fred sticks in the tree and Mikey here puts the dirt back in dat 'ole. Now, just because Fred is sick today, that don't mean that Mikey and me ain't gonna get paid."

One day a Newfie goes hunting in Alberta and manages to bag himself three ducks. He puts them in the back of his truck and is about to drive away when he is confronted by a game warden.

The game warden orders the Newfie to show his hunting licence, so the Newfie pulls out a valid Alberta hunting licence.

The warden looks at the licence, then reaches over and picks up one of the ducks, sniffs its butt and says, "This duck ain't from Alberta. This is a BC duck. Do you happen to have a BC licence?"

The Newfie reaches into his wallet and produces a BC hunting licence. The game warden looks at it, verifies that it's legal and then reaches over and grabs the second duck, sniffs its butt and says, "This surely isn't a duck from BC or Alberta. This duck is all the way from Quebec. I suppose you also have a licence from there?"

The Newfie reaches into his wallet and once again produces the correct hunting licence.

The game warden gets angry with the Newfie and yells, "Son, no one has that many licences just sitting around. Where the hell are you from?"

The Newfie gets out of his truck, turns around, drops his pants, bends over and says, "Buddy, looks like you're the expert on this one. You tell me!"

A Newfie goes duck hunting with two of his friends from the mainland. One of the mainlanders is overconfident in his ability to hunt. He tells his friends he hunts so much that he has to bring his hunting dog to catch the ducks he shoots.

After he's finished boasting, the three men split up and agree to meet back at the truck for lunch.

Noon rolls around, and the three friends gather at the truck. The Newfie is carrying no less than five ducks, and the other mainlander has managed to shoot a respectable three ducks, but the over-confident hunter stands empty-handed.

The mainlander who shot three ducks looks at his friend who hasn't shot one duck and asks, "What the hell happened to you? Don't tell me you haven't shot anything all day."

The Newfie looks over at his duckless friend and says, "Buddy, perhaps you isn't throwing the dog high enough."

CHAPTER THREE

Townies Against Baymen

A Newfie joke book wouldn't be complete if it didn't mention the rivalry between townies and baymen. The townies believe they are sophisticated city folk and that baymen are the rednecks of the island. Baymen think they live in God's country and that townies are nothing but uppity snobs who visit their cabins on the weekends. Oh, how they clash…!

A bayman and a townie are lost at sea in a small boat. They are out of food and water and are scared of dying. Each of them prays to Jesus for a miracle, but instead of getting rescued, the devil appears.

The devil says to the two Newfies, "If you can give me a task that is impossible for me to do, I'll send you to heaven. But if I can do the task that you give me, you have to return with me to hell."

The townie and the bayman think about what they can demand of the devil that will get them sent to heaven. Suddenly the townie shouts, "I got it! Take the nails out of this boat without us sinking." The devil waves his hand, the nails fly from the boat and it still stays afloat. The townie hangs his head, and the devil sends him to hell.

The bayman watches as the townie disappears from the boat. He squares his shoulders and lets go

> Q: What did the wobbly bayman say when he walked into his third bar of the evening?
>
> A: Dat hurt.

of a fart so loud the devil has to cover his ears. The devil stares at him, wide-eyed, and the bayman boldly says, "Now den, pick the bones outta dat der, buddy." The devil hangs his head, waves his hand and the bayman scores his place in heaven.

When baymen Harvey and June retired, they bought a house in St. John's. They wanted to spend more time with their grandchildren, so they moved to the city, just down the street from their family. One night when June was making Harvey's lunch, she took with wonderful pains in her chest, and Harvey jumped up and called 911.

> Q: Did you hear about the bayman Rubik's Cube?
>
> A: It is white on all sides and takes two minutes to solve.

"What's your address?" asked the operator.

Harvey replied, "On Edinburgh Drive, right at the stop sign."

"How do you spell that?" the operator inquired.

"S-T-O-P," answered Harvey.

"No, sir. The street name, how do you spell the street name?" the operator asked.

Harvey was silent for a minute. "Lard jumpin' dyin'," he said. "If I drags her 'round to First Street, will you slack arses meet me there?"

Bruce from Port aux Basques is a worrier. He worries about anything and everything. His father notices Bruce's worrying is starting to get out of hand and is affecting his health, so he tries to ease his son's mind. He says, "Bruce, me son, rightly there is only two t'ings you needs to worry about."

Bruce looks at his father and asks, "What's that?"

His father says, "Is you well or is you ill."

Bruce rolls his eyes and says, "Dad, there is so much more to worry about than that: where's the fish, and is they comin' back? Will the weather be good, or will it be too dirty to fish? Just to name a few."

Q: Why don't baymen like line dancing?

A: Because the clothespins hurt their ears.

His father continues, "Well, me son, if you is well, der's nothin' to worry about. If you is ill, der is really only two t'ings to worry about: will ya be better tomorra' or will ya die."

Bruce says, "Really, Dad, that's two new things."

His father goes on and says, "If you is better, der's nothin' to worry about. If you is dead, der's two t'ings to worry about: will you see heaven or will you see hell."

Bruce tries to interrupt. "Dad, I don't think anything can be that simple."

Bruce's father smiles at his son. "If you goes to heaven, you've got nothin' to worry about. If ya goes to hell, all you'll have to do is shake hands wit yer friends—no time for worrying."

Did You Hear...

About the townie who died while learning how to ice-fish? He got run over by the Zamboni.

About the bayman terrorist? He tried to blow up a car and burned his lips on the tailpipe.

About the bayman who wanted his buddies to help shingle his house? He put a case of beer on the roof and waited for them to show up.

About the two townies who fell asleep in a field around the bay? One got cold and told his friend to close the gate.

About the townie who put empty beer bottles in his fridge? They were for his friends who didn't drink.

A townie and a bayman are sitting side-by-side in a bar, and they both order a beer from the bartender. Each of their beers arrive with a fly floating in the foam. The townie looks at his beer disgustedly, pushes away the glass and says to the bartender, "Excuse me, my good man, but there's a fly in my beer, I'd like another." The bartender pours him another beer, and the townie happily starts drinking his pint.

The bayman looks at his beer, fishes out the fly, grabs it by the wings and starts shaking it over the glass and yells, "By the lardy jumpin' Jesus, spit it out, spit it out!"

An outport boy and his father are on a rare trip to St. John's for a doctor's appointment. They end up inside the Health Sciences Centre, staring at the elevator doors. They watch as the doors open, people get in and the doors close. When the doors open again, different people get out. Both the man and his son are confused, and they can't figure out what is going on. Finally the son asks, "What's dis 'ere, fadder?"

The father replies, "My son, I got no idea what dis contraption is. I never seen anyt'ing like it in me whole life."

At that moment, an elderly lady in a wheel-chair rolls up to the doors. She sits patiently, waits for the doors to open and rolls into the elevator as the doors close behind her. The man and his son watch as the numbers go up, stop for a minute and then come back down again. When the doors open, a beautiful young woman steps out and walks past the father and son. The man stands slack-jawed, staring at the gorgeous woman. He pushes his son toward the doors of the hospital and whispers, "Go to the truck and get yer mudder, me son!"

Q: Why do townies buy ice at Dominion?

A: They lost the recipe to make it at home.

Buddy from Little Heart's Ease sees a sign at the Irving Big Stop—"Happy Hour Special: Lobster

Tail and Beer." He looks over at his wife and says, "Lordy jumpin' Moses, me tree favourite t'ings all in one spot!"

A bayman roofer walks casually into a doctor's clinic in St. John's and speaks to the receptionist. She politely asks him what he has.

"Shingles," the bayman replies. She tells him to have a seat, so he sits down and waits for someone else to talk to him.

Fifteen minutes later, an assistant comes out and takes his name, address and MCP number. She tells him to sit tight and wait.

Another 15 minutes pass before a nurse's aide comes out and asks him what he has. Again the bayman replies, "Shingles."

Q: How did the bayman tell the townie to kill a worm?

A: Bury it.

The aide takes the roofer's complete medical history and brings him to wait in the examination room. More than half an hour later, a nurse walks in and asks him what he has. Again the bayman replies, "Shingles." The nurse takes his blood pressure, sends him for a blood test and tells him to return the next day.

The bayman shows up bright and early the next morning; this time he seems more anxious than the day before. He gives his name to the receptionist and is taken to a room where he is told to remove his clothes and wait for the doctor. Slightly confused, he strips down to his birthday suit and cautiously puts on the offered johnny coat. After waiting for more than an hour, the bayman starts to get pretty nervous and begins to pace around the room. The doctor finally shows up, and the doctor asks him—again—why he's there. Once more the bayman replies, "Shingles."

"Where?" asks the doctor.

"Out in de truck," the bayman says. "Where do ye want 'em?"

You Might Be a Bayman if...

✔ Your idea of a rock concert is Buddy Wasisname and the Other Fellers in the local stadium.

✔ A traffic jam is caused by three cars waiting for your buddy to get his boat onto the slip.

✔ The distance from the bay to town is measured in time.

✔ You bar-hop from the Legion to the Lion's Club.

✔ Most of the people you know have hit a moose at least once.

✔ You know almost all the people in your community and are probably related to a good many of them.

✔ You know of only four spices: salt, pepper, ketchup and Mt. Scio Savory.

✔ When there is nothing in your mailbox, you go into the post office and ask if the cheques have come in yet.

✔ You can buy your groceries, beer and smokes from the same gas station.

✔ You grew up believing that corn on the cob came from a can.

✔ You think broccoli is an exotic vegetable.

You Might Be a Townie if...

✔ You've seen all the biggest Canadian rock stars—10 years after they were popular in Toronto.

✔ You poke fun at baymen but spend every weekend at your cabin around the bay.

✔ Rush hour is four cars stopped at a light on the Arterial Road.

✔ You compare the gang situation in Buckmaster's Circle to the news coming from big cities on the mainland.

✔ You are happy they built the Outer Ring Road. Now you don't have to give directions to the airport to all of the baymen going to Fort McMurray.

✔ You consider anything east of the overpass "around the bay."

✔ You recognize all the new baymen going to university by their brand new clothes and really white sneakers.

✔ You do your darnedest to talk without a Newfie accent, even though we all know you have a townie accent anyway.

There is a curling competition scheduled in Nova Scotia, and the two best teams in Newfoundland are selected to compete. One team is made up entirely of townies and the other of baymen. In an attempt to save money, the economical townies hire a double-decker bus to take both teams from the ferry in North Sydney to Halifax. The townies are having a grand old time partying on the lower level of the bus when they realize they haven't heard anything from the baymen upstairs. They can't figure out what's wrong with the baymen, so they go upstairs to investigate.

Q: Why was the townie collecting burned-out light bulbs?

A: He needed them for his darkroom.

When the townies get upstairs, all the baymen are sitting straight as pokers in their seats and looking scared out of their wits. The townies call out, "What's wrong with you guys? We're having a lot of fun downstairs, and we haven't heard so much as a word from up here. We know you brought beer with you, but you haven't touched a single drop."

One of the baymen looks up and whispers, "Yes, b'y, but you got a driver..."

One winter in an isolated outport up on the Northern Peninsula, a woman goes into labour. The doctor is called in, and he arrives in the middle of the night just as the baby is about to be born. But, the minute the doctor walks through the door, the power goes out and the entire house is dark.

The father lights all the lamps and candles he can find, but the doctor can hardly see his hand in front of his face. The doctor passes the father a flashlight to provide the light needed for the birth. It only takes a few minutes before a baby boy is born. The father goes to turn off the light, but the doctor says, "Don't be too quick with that light, son, I think there's another one coming." Within minutes, a baby girl is born.

The father is dumbfounded, but goes to turn off the light again. "No, no," calls the doctor, "I think I see another one."

The father looks astonished. "By God," he says, "do you think it's the light that's attractin' 'em?"

While driving back from a weekend at his cabin, a townie accidentally ends up with his car in the ditch. He can't get any cell phone reception and is pretty sure that it's too far to walk to the next town. After sitting in his car for more than an hour, the townie notices an old man walking beside a horse, coming toward him.

The man offers to help pull out the townie with his horse, Buddy.

The man hitches Buddy up to the car and yells, "Pull, Bessie, pull!" Buddy doesn't move an inch. The townie looks puzzled.

Then the man calls out, "Pull, Nellie, pull!" Nothing happens again. The townie is going to point out that the man has called the horse Bessie and Nellie, not Buddy, but he wisely keeps his mouth shut.

Then the man screams, "Pull, Rocky, pull!" Buddy the horse still doesn't move a muscle.

The man walks up to Buddy and whispers in the horse's ear, "Pull, Buddy, pull." Buddy easily pulls the car out of the ditch.

The townie's curiosity is piqued by what he has just witnessed, so he decides to ask the man about it. "Sir, you said the horse's name is Buddy, but you yelled out to Bessie, Nellie and Rocky before you asked Buddy to pull. How did that work?" The man replies, "Well, see, Buddy here is blind, and if he even thought he was pullin' alone, I'm sure he wouldn't have even bothered to try."

Q: How many baymen does it take to screw in a light bulb?

A: Eleven. One to hold the light bulb and 10 to drink 'til the room spins.

A bayman gets piss-drunk in a pub on George Street. Eventually he leaves the pub, and as he staggers down the street, he walks right into a light pole. He feels his way around the entire pole and then sits down on the sidewalk with a thump. He is there for a good 15 minutes until his friend staggers by and shouts, "Hey, buddy, is you comin' to the next pub? The b'ys is already orderin' the beers!"

The bayman looks at his friend and replies, "It's no use, b'y. I can't get outta here. I'm boxed in."

The Bayman Calendar

January: Spend whole month cutting wood.

February: Spend half the month ice fishing and spend other half hauling wood from last year.

March: Give up salt for Lent. Take three hours before breaking the Easter promise.

April: Manage to go ice fishing until the middle of month. Quad only goes through ice once.

May: Prepare for first camping trip of the year. Spend weekend in tent during a snowstorm.

June: Wait for summer to arrive. It doesn't show up 'til August.

July: Think summer is coming, but it's only nippers and flies.

August: Summer arrives, and for those two weeks the weather is perfect for trouting.

September: Spend month splitting wood for the winter. Force youngsters to pile it in the basement. Start building bonfire for Bonfire Night.

October: Go moose hunting. Shoot at three, miss all three, throw gun in pond and curse damn moose. Send kids out jannying with bedsheet costumes. Let them eat all the candy. They are sick for days.

NOVEMBER: Have great Bonfire Night. Catch woods on fire and call volunteer fire department. Order everything for Christmas from Sears catalogue.

DECEMBER: Go to post every day asking about parcels sent from Fort McMurray. Spend Christmas Eve mummering around town.

Ken, a bayman who works at the local fish plant, accidentally cuts off all 10 of his fingers. He is rushed to the emergency room of the Health Sciences Centre.

The doctor walks up to Ken's bed and asks, "'Kay, me son, where are ya fingers at?"

Ken quickly responds, "B'y, I 'aven't got 'em 'ere. Left 'em at da plant."

Q: How many baymen does it take to fill in a pothole?

A: Three—one to fill in the pothole and two to make sure that it looks like they are all doing work.

The doctor is surprised at Ken's answer and says, "My God, b'y. Ya should've brought them along. We might have been able to save them for ya. This is the Health Sciences Centre, we works miracles here."

Ken looks at the doctor and explains, "Well, den, 'ow the 'ell was I s'posed to pick 'em up?"

The Townie Calendar

JANUARY: After holidays, go on vacation in Florida.

FEBRUARY: Plan romantic Valentine's Day at Delta Hotel; get nothing in return.

MARCH: Give up shopping for Lent. Break down and buy groceries.

APRIL: Plan an Easter egg hunt in park. Find Easter eggs from last year. Children eat them and are sick for two days.

MAY: Prepare for first camping trip of the year. Spend weekend in RV during a snow-storm.

JUNE: Wait for summer to arrive. It doesn't show up 'til August. Tell everyone who lives on mainland that it has been summertime for weeks.

JULY: Spend every weekend at cabin pretending to live like a bayman.

AUGUST: Cheer on rowers at Regatta Day. Thankful for holiday.

SEPTEMBER: Send children back to school. Acknowledge summer was only two weeks in August.

OCTOBER: Buy Halloween costumes at Wal-Mart, and send children trick-or-treating at the mall. Divide candy into 12 piles so they won't eat it all at once. Listen to children complain.

> **NOVEMBER:** Buy Christmas presents at Avalon Mall. Get into fistfight over parking space near the Intermission.
>
> **DECEMBER:** Put up Christmas lights. Drive around St. John's comparing other lights to mine. Decide mine are best, and write letter to *Evening Telegram* to tell them so.

To get away from their high-stress jobs, a couple from St. John's likes to spend relaxing weekends in their motor home. But every single weekend, the couple finds their peace and quiet disturbed by friendly visits from mainlanders staying in the park. The tourists ask the couple incessant questions about Newfoundland.

Q: Why are there no jokes about Mount Pearl?

A: Because the townies find it too hard to think of them.

It takes several weekends, but the man and woman eventually come up with a plan to make sure they get some privacy.

The next time they go to camp, they place a sign on the door of their motor home:

"Insurance agent. Ask about our term-life package."

A drunk bayman is stumbling home one day when he gets lost and finds himself in the bush. He falls to the ground and notices a lamp. He picks it up, rubs it and out comes a genie. "You have three wishes, choose them wisely," says the genie.

The bayman looks down at his last, and empty, bottle of Black Horse, smashes it on a rock and says, "I wants a beer that will never, ever run out. I needs it to always be cold and ready to drink."

Q: How many townies does it take to go ice fishing?

A: Four—one to cut the hole and three to push the boat through.

"No problem," says the genie, "but remember, you are the only one who can drink beer from the bottle."

A bottle appears in front of the bayman. He takes a swig of the beer—it's perfect. He downs the whole thing, and before he can set the empty bottle down, it's full again. The bayman is happy as a lark and starts to walk away.

"Where are you going?" asks the genie. "You still have two wishes left!"

"Well, den," replies the bayman, "pass along two more of these!"

Frankie walks into a bar in Conception Bay South. On the door there's a sign that reads, "If you can make my horse laugh, I'll give you $50."

Frankie walks up to the bartender and says, "Buddy, I can make your horse laugh."

He goes out behind the bar and is gone for about 10 minutes. When he comes back in, the horse is laughing so loudly everyone can hear it. The bartender hands over $50.

About three months later, Frankie comes back into the bar, but this time the sign reads, "If you can make my horse cry, I'll give you $50."

Frankie walks up to the bartender and says, "I can make your horse cry."

He walks out behind the bar and is gone for about 15 minutes. When he comes back, everyone in the bar can hear the horse crying. The bartender agrees to pay Frankie the $50 on one condition: he wants to know how Frankie has made a horse laugh and cry.

Frankie boasts to the whole bar, "To make him laugh, I told him my willy is bigger than his. To make him cry, I showed him!"

Q: What does a bayman call a boat out in the harbour?

A: Luh.

Q: What does a bayman call a boat full of fish tied up beside the wharf?

A: Luh luh.

Q: What does a bayman call a boat that was full of fish but capsized and dumped all the fish?

A: Awww, luh.

A townie is driving through a small community around the bay, and he runs over a rabbit. He isn't sure what happened, so he stops the car in front of bayman Willy's house and gets out to take a look. As he is standing there, looking at the dead rabbit,

Willy pulls into his driveway. The bayman walks over to the townie and asks what's going on.

The townie says, "I'm just passing through your community and I seem to have killed a rabbit right outside your front door."

Willy looks down, sees the dead rabbit and says, "No problem, b'y. Give me a second."

Willy goes to his truck and returns with a spray can. He empties it over the rabbit, tosses the can into the ditch and says, "There ya go, buddy. Enjoy yer drive." He walks into his house and closes the door.

> Q: How can you tell if a Newfie grew up using an outhouse?
>
> A: He likes the winter catalogue better because it has fur coats in it.
>
> He saves the tissue paper from apples and oranges for further use.
>
> He keeps his boots at the ready for midnight walks.
>
> He learns to aim in the dark.

The townie turns to walk away, but suddenly the rabbit gets up, hops 10 feet, turns around and waves, hops 10 feet more, turns around and waves, hops 10 feet more and disappears into the woods with one last wave at the townie.

The townie is astounded. He has no idea what the bayman did to fix the dead rabbit. He takes the can out of the ditch and reads the label. It says: "Hairspray. Guaranteed to bring dead hair back to life with a permanent wave."

One day a bayman goes down to see Garge, the best carpenter in their small town. He asks Garge to make him a wooden crate that is one inch tall, one inch wide and 50 feet long.

When Garge asks what the bayman needs the crate for, he replies "Lard Jesus, yesterday the wife snapped her clothesline, and now I needs to send it all the way to Toronto to get it fixed."

Two townies meet a bayman in a pub on George Street. The b'ys leave the bar completely drunk, and an RNC officer catches the three men peeing on the sidewalk. They pull up their flies and take off running. The officer starts chasing them, yelling for the men to stop.

The trio darts behind Ziggy Peelgoods and spies three empty potato sacks on the ground. They each climb into a sack just as the officer catches up with them.

The officer kicks the first sack, and one of the townies calls out, "Meow!"

The officer figures it's just a stray cat and kicks the second bag.

The next townie calls out, "Woof!"

Figuring it's just a stray dog, the officer moves on and kicks the third bag.

Q: What did the townie bus driver say to the passenger with no legs?
A: "How ya getting on?"

The bayman has no idea what to do, so he calls out, "Po-ta-to!"

All three men end up spending the night in the drunk-tank.

Sally, a blonde from St. John's, is going on her first camping trip with her daughter's Girl Guide group. Sally's husband Brad, from around the bay, tries to teach her everything she needs to know about camping, but he isn't sure if she understands a word he's saying. One of the most important rules to remember before setting out, he tells her, is to make sure to test out all the gear—it can be disastrous to get into the woods and find out that something doesn't work or is broken.

Q: Did you hear what the St. John's city council wrote on the bottom of the community swimming pool?

A: No smoking.

While on the trip, Sally follows her husband's instructions, gets everyone together and assigns different duties to each Girl Guide.

Jennifer is in charge of the food supplies, Carla is the cook, Lisa is responsible for the maps and making up a time schedule, Stacey is to decide on the group's events and Sally, the leader, is supposed to test all the gear.

They get to the campsite and everyone is excited. The group arrives right on schedule and is getting ready for their first event—hiking through the woods—but they want to eat first. Sally asks Carla if she will prepare the meal and, of course, Carla says she will.

About 10 minutes later, Carla comes back and tells Sally, "I can't make the supper, miss. I can't light a fire with the matches you brought."

Sally replies, "I don't understand! Those matches should work perfectly. I tested them all just before we left."

A blind townie and his guide dog enter a pub and find their way to a bar stool.

After ordering a drink and sitting down for a while, the townie yells to the entire bar, "Hey, does anyone want to hear a bayman joke?"

The bar immediately goes dead quiet.

Then, in the sexiest voice the townie has ever heard, the woman next to him says, "Before you tell that joke, I'm going to give you some information. The bartender is a bayman, the owner is a bayman and the bouncer is a six-foot-tall, 220-pound bayman with a black belt in karate. What's more, the man sitting next to me is bayman and a fisherman. He can lift 200 pounds without even thinking about it. Think about it seriously. Do you still wanna tell that bayman joke?"

Q: Did you hear about the bayman who put his condom on inside out?

A: He didn't come, he went.

The blind guy says, "Nah, not if I'm gonna have to explain it four times."

A bayman is working as a carpet-fitter in St. John's. One day, as he finishes up a job, he gets a powerful craving for a cigarette.

The bayman looks all around and discovers that his cigarettes are missing. He checks in his pockets and even goes out to his truck and searches for them, but they are nowhere to be found. Going back inside, he notices a bump in the carpet and figures he has laid the carpet over the pack without noticing it was there.

He looks around to make sure no one is watching, and decides rather than pull up the carpet, he'll grab a hammer and pound the pack into the floor so no one will know it's there. When the bayman finishes getting rid of the traces of the package of cigarettes, the owner of the house walks into the room and comments on what a wonderful job the carpet-fitter has done.

Q: Why is it always good to drive with a bayman in the passenger seat?

A: You can always park in a handicapped spot.

"The carpet looks great!" the owner exclaims. "Here are your cigarettes; I found them in the kitchen. Have you seen my cell phone?"

The Government of Newfoundland has set up a space agency in St. John's. In order to get hired, you have to pass a test showing how much you know about the history of space exploration.

The first applicant, a townie, writes that the Russians were the first in space. The second applicant, a bayman, writes that the Americans were the first to land on the moon. Both of them are correct, so the manager asks the pair to speculate on what each of them can bring to space exploration.

The bayman stands up and announces that Newfoundland can be the first group to land on the sun.

The townie shouts out, "You can't land on the sun, you idiot! You'll burn up!"

The bayman quickly replies, "We're not that stunned, b'y. We're going at night!"

A fisherman from town is out on the pond, trouting in a small boat, when he notices a bayman in a small boat open his tackle box and take out a mirror. Curious, the townie rows over and asks, "Excuse me, what is the mirror for?"

"Dat's my secret way to catch fish," says the bayman. "Shine dis here looking glass on the top of the water, the fishes notices the spot of light and as God as my witness, they swim to the surface. Then

I just reaches down with a net and pulls them into the boat."

"Wow! Does that really work?" the townie asks.

The bayman replies, "It sure do, b'y."

"Would you be interested in selling that mirror?" asks the townie. "I'll give you $30 for it."

"Well, okay," says the bayman. "Jus' promise me you won't go off telling anyone else me secret."

After the money is transferred, the townie asks, "By the way, how many fish have you caught this week?"

"You is the sixth one," the bayman laughs.

How can you tell if a Newfie is a true bayman? He lives in a town with a sexual connotation, he is proud as punch to be from there and he gets a kick out of telling the name of his hometown to everyone he meets.

A bayman walks through the front door of a bar. He is obviously drunk as he staggers up to the bar, manages to seat himself upright on a stool and ask the bartender for a drink. The bartender politely informs the bayman that it appears he has already had plenty to drink, and that he will not be served any more liquor at the bar but they will gladly call him a cab.

The bayman is surprised, but he climbs down off the bar stool and stumbles out the front door. A few minutes later, the same drunk bayman crashes in the side door of the same bar. He wobbles up to a bar stool and hollers for a drink. The bartender comes over and firmly refuses to serve the man. Again the bartender kindly offers to call a cab for the bayman.

The drunk eyes the bartender, angrily curses and heads out the side door.

A few minutes later, the same bayman bursts in through the back door of the bar. He plops himself down on a bar stool, takes a minute to figure out where he is and demands a drink from the bartender.

The bartender comes over and reminds the bayman that he is obviously drunk and won't get any more

Q: Why did the bayman put condoms on his ears?

A: He didn't want to get hearing aids.

drinks for the rest of the night. He now has two choices: let the bartender call a cab or else he will call the police immediately.

The bayman clears his head, looks up at the bartender and says, "Holy mother of God, man! How many bars does you work at around here, anyways?"

The boss of a fish plant around the bay happens to be a townie. One day, he realizes that he never gets any respect from the baymen who work at the plant. The townie knows he's capable of helping the workers make more money with less effort, but no one who works in the plant will listen to him.

The next day, the townie brings in a small sign and sticks it on his office door. The sign reads: "I'm the boss."

Later that day when he returns from his lunch break, the townie sees that someone has taped a note underneath the sign that says: "Buddy, your wife called about 10 minutes ago. She wants her sign back!"

Q: How did the bayman break his leg while raking leaves?

A: He fell out of the tree.

Robbie and Mike have been friends and drinking buddies for years. They have

grown up together and figure they will die in the same small town around the bay that they were born in. After having a few drinks one night, Mike says to Robbie, "Robbie, b'y, we have been friends for a really long time, luh, and if I dies afore you, could you honour me last wish? Get the coldest dozen bottles of Black Horse you can find and upend 'em over my grave."

Robbie replies, "Mike, my son, I would be down-right glad to do dat for you, my old friend. But how would you feel if I ran that beer through me own bladder first?"

CHAPTER FOUR

Quirky Geography

There aren't many Canadians who haven't heard about the infamous and sometimes-odd naming conventions used in Newfoundland. It's true that people don't often believe the names are real. Well, they are, and I can vouch for them, embarrassing or not...

The Newfie Town Alphabet

A is for Ass Hill. Certainly not climbed by Jack and Jill.

B is for Bacon Cove. A place where everyone has a stove.

C is for Come By Chance. Where men don't often drop their pants.

D is for Dildo. For women with a high libido.

E is for Exploits River. Grab your pole, go ahead and give 'er.

F is for Funk Lake. Sure to cure your heart's ache.

G is for Goobies. A favourite truck stop without boobies.

H is for Heart's Content. A visit here, you won't regret.

I is for Isle aux Morts. Deadman's island, 'tis nuthin' of the sort.

J is for Jerry's Nose. For a picture here, you must pose.

K is for King's Point. A royal visit, on that you can count.

L is for Leading Tickles. Where the weather is quite fickle.

M is for Mosquito. A stay here, you won't veto.

N is for Neddy Harbour. Can't be confused with Petty Harbour.

O is for Old Man's Head. Leaving here? Sure you'd rather be dead.

P is for Paradise. The people here are rather nice.

Q is for Quidi Vidi. Stop in here for a short randy.

R is for Ramea. Activities here might cause some drama.

S is for Stag Harbour. Women here are loved with ardour.

T is for Too Good Arm. Trouble here is cause for alarm.

U is for Upper Island Cove. Where tourists, they show up in droves.

V is for Virgin Arm. The women here are never calm.

W is for Witless Bay. Their schooling lessons never stay.

Y is for York Harbour. For the crown, they often labour.

Our alphabet has come to a head, but you may have noticed there's no *X* or *Z*. We clearly named our towns for fun, but those two letters we had to shun.

Newfie Town Names Sure to Raise an Eyebrow

BLOW ME DOWN: Okay, this one was named for the wind that howls off the coast, but mainlanders don't need to know that.

COME BY CHANCE: Women don't want to date men from here, and men don't want to admit they are from here. Oh, and it has an oil refinery.

CONCEPTION BAY: Well, we did need to populate an entire province through fishermen who travelled here from England...

DILDO: Whether it was named after the shape of the headland, a cactus, the pegs that hold oars to a dory or an artificial penis, tourists still steal the signs, line up to have their picture taken with Captain Dildo and have their passports stamped at the local post office. Also, Canada Post lets offices that still hand-cancel their letters design the cancellation mark. Some of the more common marks for the province are boats and whales and items that generally represent Newfoundland. But what was the suggestion for the post office located in Dildo? A big happy face.

OLD MAN'S HEAD: Get your mind out of the gutter. The "head" refers to the most prominent land in an area. Take a look at the shape of your grandfather's head. Compare it to the land around you. Any similarities?

SOUTH DILDO: Yes, you got it right; it is south of the town of Dildo.

SPREAD EAGLE: It might be named for the bird, but who really knows?

VIRGIN ARM: This is a community entirely populated by children.

Baytona? I Mean Gayside. I Mean Where?

The town officials of a small outport town called Gayside actually got together in 1985 and decided the town name was too offensive. They put together a campaign, kind of like the Pepsi commercials, featuring rock stars who could help change the offensive name. The whole town voted for Baytona in place of Gayside. The name change went off without a hitch, and all the residents were happy with Baytona. The whole renaming thing, however, produced an inadvertent side effect—no one knew where Baytona was. Tourists and Newfies alike were asking where it was located and the answer most often given was, "You know, that town that used to be called Gayside." Not exactly helpful.

Inspired by Gayside/Baytona, the same name-changing idea also found a brief foothold in the small community of Dildo, arguably one of the more notable towns in Newfoundland. The locals fought it, though. If the name was changed, what would everyone call Dildo Days, Dildo Dollars and Captain Dildo?

Newfie Town Names that Make You Cry

Everyone thinks Newfie towns are all named after something funny. Not so. Some of the names here are the most depressing in the country.

GRIPE POINT: Not the happiest of people here.

FAMINE POINT: We all don't stock up on Jam Jams for the winter.

BLEAK ISLAND: Not picturesque in any way, shape or form.

MISERY POINT: Probably named after the winters on the island.

EMPTY BASKET: The Easter Bunny never manages to get here.

BLEAK JOKE COVE: This one was probably named after all the really bad Newfie jokes that get told throughout Canada.

Newfie Town Names that Make You Yawn

Some of Newfoundland's town names took a lot of imagination, but some were named without much thought at all.

PLATE COVE: I guess the settlers really liked dinner.

LADLE COVE: These settlers must have loved gravy. Perhaps it all comes from France where *le sauce est tout* ("the sauce," or in this case "the gravy," "is everything").

DEEP BAY: I'm gonna guess that bay is deep. But that's only a guess.

Newfie Town Names that Make You Growl

Newfies also like to name their towns after animals, and these names are more creative than most.

LION'S DEN: Trust me when I tell you, lions are not native to the island.

DRAGON BAY: Nope, we don't secretly breed dragons for Harry Potter.

MOUSE ISLAND: There has to be a lot of mice on an island to make this name stick.

PIGEON ISLAND: How many pigeons does an island have to harbour before it gets named after the bird that inhabits it?

GULL ISLAND: Well, this one is probably accurate. Newfoundland is lousy with gulls of all kinds.

HERRING NECK: Next time you're looking at a herring, try and point out its neck. I bet you can't find it.

Newfie Town Names: Honourable Mentions

Ass Rock
Badger
Bar Haven
Billy Butts Pond
Cape Onion
Coffee Cove
Cow Head
Cupids
Deadman's Bay
Diamond Cove
Fortune
Furby's Cove
Gin Cove
Goblin
Halfway Point
Happy Adventure
Ivanhoe
Keels
Lawn
Little Seldom
Low Point
Nippers Harbour
Noggin Cove
Old Room
Poor Boy Island
Red Indian Lake
Salvage
Seldom
St. Jones Within
St. Jones Without
Wild Bight

CHAPTER FIVE

Newfoundland Versus Canada— and Everywhere in Between

For many years, Newfies have been the butt of jokes told from Halifax to Vancouver, and the rumour has persisted that we are the ones who make up the jokes in the first place. Well, that may be true (I won't admit anything), but we also make sure we have a strong hand in poking fun at mainlanders. For us, you see, it's not that hard to think of ways to laugh at Torontonians or Albertans; they just make it so darned easy…

A Torontonian wants to become a Newfie. He goes to several specialists in Toronto and asks them if there is anything they can do to turn him into a Newfie. Each doctor looks at the Torontonian like he's crazy and tells him to get lost.

He then gets the bright idea of trying the doctors in Newfoundland, and the last specialist he visits gives him hope.

The specialist says, "Sure, that's easy. All I have to do is remove one-third of your brain, and poof! You'll be as Newfie as they come."

The Torontonian decides to have the procedure, but while the specialist is operating his hand slips and he cuts out two-thirds of the Torontonian's brain instead of the one-third he originally intended to.

The specialist has no idea what state his patient is going to be in when he wakes up, so the doctor stays by the Torontonian's bedside all night.

When the patient comes to, the doctor starts to explain what went wrong. He tells the man how the scalpel slipped and that the damage is irreversible.

The Torontonian stares blankly at the doctor and says, *"Je ne comprends pas, monsieur."*

A Newfie driving way over the Highway 401 speed limit in Ontario gets pulled over.

After asking for his licence, registration and insurance, the OPP officer asks the Newfie, "Do you have any idea what speed we clocked you at?"

The Newfie stops for a minute, looks strangely at the officer and replies, "No, sir. I got no idea how fast I was going that time."

The officer doesn't like how the Newfie is staring at him, so he asks what the Newfie is looking at.

The Newfie smiles and says, "B'y, it looks to me like you got yerself a circle fly."

The officer asks what a circle fly is.

"My God, sure everyone knows what that is," replies the Newfie. "It's the fly that circles 'round a horse's arse. Them horses waves their tails 'round and 'round tryin' to get rid of them."

The officer is angry now, and says, "Sir, are you calling me a horse's ass?"

The Newfie shakes his head and answers, "No, sir, I'm not callin' you anything of the sort, but by God, there's no way yet that you can fool a circle fly."

An Albertan and a Newfie are seated beside each other on an airplane bound for Las Vegas. They are about two hours into the flight, and suddenly the plane lurches to the right. The pilot comes on the intercom

Q: What's black and blue and found lying in a ditch?

A: A mainlander who told too many Newfie jokes.

and announces the airplane just lost an engine but everything is all right. He lets everyone know there are three more engines, but the flight will take about an hour longer than expected.

Half an hour later, the plane lurches again, but this time everything shifts to the left. The pilot gets on the intercom and informs the passengers the airplane has lost one of the left-side engines. He lets everyone know that it's going to be okay, and that there are still two more engines, but the most recent setback will add another hour to the flight.

Suddenly the Albertan says loudly, "For goodness sake, if we lose the last two engines, we'll be up here all day!"

While sitting in a bar, George, a Newfie, and Danny, an Albertan, get into an argument about who has the higher intelligence level. The b'ys argue back and forth, and Danny bets George that for every question he can't answer he will give Danny five dollars. Danny sweetens the deal by telling George that any questions Danny himself can't answer will earn George $50. George quickly accepts the bet.

Danny asks the first question: "Which star is closest to Earth?"

George slowly shakes his head and passes over five dollars. He has no idea which star is closest to Earth.

George takes his turn: "What walks up a hill on three legs and walks down the same hill on four?"

Danny thinks for a long time. He makes several calls and can't figure out the answer. He pulls out his laptop and looks on the Internet—nothing. After two hours of searching, he has to admit defeat. He passes over $50, and he isn't happy about it.

Still, Danny is so amazed he has been outsmarted by a Newfie that he has to find out the answer to the question.

He asks George, "Well, what's the answer? What walks up a hill on three legs and walks down the same hill on four?"

George doesn't say a word and hands over five dollars.

10 Tips for Surviving a Trip to Newfoundland

1. Memorize every joke about Newfoundland that you can find. When visiting the province, tell everyone you meet at least one of your jokes. We love it when you prove to us how much research you've done about Newfoundland.

2. Refer to every Newfoundlander and Labradorian as a Newfie. This will make you feel like you fit in.

3. When interacting with people who are from Newfoundland and Labrador, stick to topics that are well-known conversation starters, such as "Is unemployment still high in Newfoundland?" Or, "My brother Phil works with a Newfie in Fort McMurray."

4. Learn the correct pronunciation of Newfoundland. People might tell you that it rhymes with "understand," but that's not true. The correct way to pronounce Newfoundland is "Newfinlin" (the faster you say it, the easier it is for us to understand).

5. Use as much slang as you can. As a last resort, add "b'y" to the end of every sentence.

6. Plan your trip around *This Hour Has 22 Minutes*. Newfoundlanders never miss an episode. We close shops and tourist attractions when

(10 Tips cont.)

it is on. This holds true for the *Rick Mercer Report* and old reruns of *Codco*.

7. The only drink available in any bar is Screech. Don't bother asking for anything else. Sure, you will see other bottles in the bar, but they are just for show. Someone sent them home from Fort McMurray.

8. Always comment on the weather. We love it when tourists point out the obvious lack of sun and abundance of rain and fog.

9. Remember that our restaurants are only open when they have fish to serve. This doesn't happen very often since the cod fishery collapsed. Better to be safe than sorry, and bring all your necessary provisions yourself. These include, but are not limited to, fresh water, gasoline, vegetables and garbage bags.

10. Be amazed at the prosperity of the locals. Every time you see a new car, make sure you point it out. If you see a new house being built, let everyone know you think it's marvellous that people don't have to live in shacks by the ocean anymore.

At the top of the CN Tower, a Newfie is holding his watch over the edge, staring at the street below. He looks serious, and every few minutes he scribbles down some notes and goes back to staring. A tourist from Alberta asks him what he's doing.

The Newfie replies, "I'm conductin' a science experiment. I wanna know if you could drop your watch from 'ere and skitter down dem der stairs and catch it."

The Albertan laughs. "I know it isn't possible to drop your watch from the top of the CN Tower, run down and catch it. No one is that fast."

"Well," says the Newfie, "you stay put right 'ere, and we'll find out." With that, he adjusts his watch, drops it and disappears through the door.

The Albertan waits and waits. He figures the Newfie's watch was destroyed, and that he isn't returning out of embarrassment. Just as the Albertan is about to leave, the Newfie walks up, holding the watch and grinning from ear to ear.

The Albertan exclaims, "That's impossible! How did you catch it?"

"Easy," says the Newfie. "I just set the watch to Newfoundland time, back a half-hour."

A woman from BC walks into a Newfoundland flight school. She insists they teach her how to fly that day. Unfortunately, all the planes are in use, so the owner agrees to instruct the woman on how to fly a single-man helicopter. As he is going to be instructing her by radio, the owner makes sure the woman understands that she needs to stay in constant contact.

Q: Why are Newfie jokes so dumb?

A: So the rest of Canada can understand them.

The Newfie takes his student out to the helicopter, shows her the basics, explains how to start the thing and then sends her off into the wild blue yonder.

After the woman climbs to about 1000 feet, she radioes in. "I'm doing great! I love it! The view is so beautiful, and I'm really starting to get the hang of this."

At 2000 feet, she radioes in again, saying how easy it is to fly. The owner watches on the radar as she climbs to over 3000 feet. He starts to worry about her because she hasn't radioed in for a while.

A few minutes later, the instructor watches in horror as she crashes about half a kilometre away. He runs over and pulls her from the wreckage.

When he asks what happened, she says, "I don't know! Everything was going fine, but as I got higher, I was starting to get cold. I can't remember anything after I turned off the big fan."

A husband and wife from Toronto are vacationing in central Newfoundland when they see a U-pick sign. They decide to enjoy some local produce, and pull over to the side of the road. As they are walking up the dirt road to the farm, the farmer passes them with a load of manure. The smell is almost too much to bear.

The husband calls out, "Excuse me, sir, what are you carrying?"

The Newfie calls back, "Sure b'y, dis here is manure. I gets it from Daisy down de road."

The wife asks, "Well, then, what can you possibly do with manure that smells that horrible?" The Newfie says, "Sure missus, dat's for to put on the strawberries."

The wife looks at her husband and whispers, "Isn't that odd, we put whipped cream on ours."

A Newfie stands at the corner of Bay and Dundas Streets in Toronto with one thing in mind: to trick all the mainlanders he can. He starts dancing a jig on a manhole cover. He has a huge smile on his face, and every time he jumps up he yells, "Forty-four, forty-four!" Eventually he attracts a fair amount of attention, and a crowd gathers around to watch this fool dancing in Toronto.

One of the men from the crowd says, "You seem very happy, sir. Could I try dancing on that cover to see if it might cheer me up?"

The Newfie gets the man to start jumping on the manhole and calls out, "Jump up higher, me son, higher, and you got to say 'forty-four.'" The man jumps higher and starts smiling and yelling out, "Forty-four!"

Suddenly, the Newfie pulls away the manhole, and the fellow drops into the sewer. The Newfie puts the manhole cover back, and he starts jumping again, this time calling out, "Forty-five, forty-five!"

A Newfie walks into a bar on his first night in Fort McMurray. He pulls up a bar stool and sits right in front of the bartender.

The bartender asks him what he wants, and the Newfie replies, "B'y, pass me along a bottle of Black Horse and a shot of Screech."

The bartender pours the drinks and says, "Ah, a Newfie, eh? You must be out here looking for work."

The Newfie nods his head and says, "Well, me son, 'tis like this. We finished all our work at home and had to come out 'ere and finish yers."

An Albertan phones the police in a panic and happens to get the Newfie RCMP officer on duty. The Albertan explains that he needs an officer to come to his house immediately. When the officer asks what the problem is, the Albertan exclaims that someone has stolen his steering wheel, gearshift, dashboard and windshield. Even the Newfie thinks this is strange, but he has to check out the call anyway. While the officer is gathering his coat and gloves, the phone rings again, and the Albertan apologizes. "Don't bother to come over, sir; I got in the back seat by mistake."

An elderly Newfie who was a pilot in World War II is seated on a plane headed for Fort McMurray. He is going to visit his grandchildren for the first time. As the flight nears the Fort McMurray airport, the wind picks up something terrible, and the plane lands pretty hard on the runway.

As everyone gets off the plane, the captain stands beside the cockpit door, wishing everyone a good day.

The old Newfie reaches the front and says to the captain, "B'y, 'twas not a horrible flight, but we pitched something terrible. I gots one question for ya. Did we land or was we shot down?"

One day, an American walks into a bar, hits a Newfie over the head, laughs and says, "That's a karate chop from Japan."

The next day, the same American hits the same Newfie over the head and laughs, but this time he says, "That's a tae-kwon-do chop from Korea."

On the third day, the American does it again. He hits the Newfie over the head, laughs and says, "That's a kung-fu chop from China."

The next day, the Newfie isn't in the bar when the American walks in, so he sits down and orders a drink. Suddenly, everyone in the bar hears a huge WHACK! and the American falls off his stool and lands on the floor.

The Newfie smiles and says to the American, "That there is a crowbar from Canadian Tire, me son."

A mainlander walks into a restaurant in Newfoundland and asks the waiter what the day's specials are.

The Newfie waiter responds, "Our special of the day is moose tongue. Would you like to give it a try?"

The mainlander quickly says, "No, sir, I do not eat anything that comes from an animal's mouth."

The Newfie waiter tries again. "Well then, buddy, do ya want an omelette instead?"

A Newfie walks into a bank in downtown Toronto to meet with a loans officer. The Newfie explains that he's going on a trip and wants to borrow $5000. The loans officer has the Newfie fill out a bunch of papers and then says the bank requires a security deposit for this type of loan.

The Newfie reaches into his pocket, pulls out the keys to his brand new car and tosses them across the desk. The loans officer checks out the car and the title, and finds everything to be in order. He explains that the bank will hold the car until the Newfie pays back the loan with 12 percent interest. The Newfie readily agrees to the conditions and leaves the bank to start his vacation.

The bank officials have a good laugh at the Newfie for putting down a brand new car as collateral for a $5000 loan. They think it was good fun that he even agreed to leave it at the bank. They all stop laughing when the loans officer discovers that the Newfie is a millionaire. Once they see how much money he has, they can't understand why he needs the loan.

Two weeks later, the Newfie returns and pays back the loan and the interest of $23.07. Puzzled, the loans officer wants to know about the Newfie and the transaction. The loans officer politely asks, "Sir, after you left your car here, we were able to find out more about your financial situation. You didn't need the loan. Why did you ask for it?" The Newfie replies, "Us Newfies aren't as stunned as you think. Where else in Toronto can I park my car for two weeks, pay only $23.07 and know that the car will still be there when I get back?"

On a routine Air Canada flight between Toronto and Calgary, a Newfie woman sits beside her Calgarian sister-in-law. The flight has already been delayed twice because of mechanical issues, so the women are more than an hour late leaving Toronto. After the flight finally takes off, the women notice the lights flickering, so they call the attendant over and mention the problem. The attendant tells them she will take care of it. A few minutes later, the lights in the cabin are turned off; it's obvious the attendant turned the lights off to satisfy the women. The attendant comes back and asks the women if everything is okay now.

The Newfie woman looks at her sister-in-law and says, "For the love of God, don't ask her about the rattling sound coming from the engines."

A mainland tourist is chatting with an elderly Newfoundland fisherman. The tourist comments on how hard the Newfie must work to earn a living. The mainlander asks the Newfie if he has any sons to help him with his work.

The fisherman replies, "Yes, sir, I got two sons living and one in Toronto."

Late one night, a Newfie is proudly showing off his new apartment in Edmonton to a couple buddies. The last stop on the grand tour is his bedroom. He shows his friends his new king-sized bed that has a giant brass gong and a mallet sitting beside it.

"What's up with that brass gong?" asks one of the Newfie's friends.

"Sure, b'y, dat's not a gong. It's a talking clock. I had that ordered in special from St. John's," the Newfie replies.

"A talking clock? Seriously?" asks his astonished friend.

"Yup," replies the Newfie.

"How's it work?" the friend asks as he leans over and stares at the gong.

"Watch and learn, me son," the Newfie replies. He picks up the mallet, gives the gong an ear-shattering pound and steps back.

The three men stand there, looking at one another for about a minute.

Suddenly, someone on the other side of the wall screams, "You jerk! It's 3:15 in the morning!"

Marge and Garge are strolling down Yonge Street in Toronto. They pass a shop that has two guys sitting on a bench inside it. Garge looks at Marge and says, "Marge, me dear, watch this. Those two fellers in there figgers that they is smart mainlanders. I'm gonna show them."

Garge pokes his head in the door and hollers, "What you fellers sellin'?"

One of the guys in the shop looks up and calls back, "We're selling assholes. Need any?"

Garge smirks and replies, "Not today, b'ys, but it looks like business is good with only two left in the store."

A Newfie goes into a gas station restroom in Ontario. He finishes his business and walks past a mainlander carefully washing his hands. The mainlander casually comments, "Excuse me, sir, but my mother taught me that it was sanitary to always wash my hands after using the restroom."

The Newfie eyes him and quips, "Ha! Well, my mudder taught me not to piss on my hands."

CHAPTER SIX

God Bless the Newfies

Newfoundland has a long history with religion. Every town prides itself on having a church, even if the minister can only attend sporadically. Traditionally, the province has been split between Roman Catholics and Protestants, and as everyone knows, these two groups have been at odds since they left Europe and landed on the island. But while there have been many scuffles between the Catholics and the Protestants on The Rock, we Newfies have never actually engaged in an all-out war between religions. The Protestants just continue to poke fun at the Catholics and their bingos, and the Catholics just try to ignore everything that doesn't come from the pope.

A Sunday school teacher wants to figure out if her students understand what it takes to get into heaven. She asks them if selling her house and her car and giving all of her money to the church will get her into heaven. All of the children shout, "No!"

She asks if taking care of the church, mowing the lawn and making supper for the priest every day will get her into heaven. Again all of the children shout, "No!"

She asks them if being kind to animals, giving candy to children and feeding the poor and hungry will get her into heaven. Again all of the children shout, "No!"

At this point the teacher isn't sure if they know the answer she wants, so she asks them to tell her what she needs to do to make sure she ends up in heaven. The children are all silent until one boy says, "Well, I figures you gotta be dead, miss."

A Newfie man dies and manages to end up in heaven. As he stands in front of the Pearly Gates waiting to enter, he sees a wall of clocks behind St. Peter.

When it's the man's turn at the gates, he looks at St. Peter and asks, "Buddy, what's all them clocks for?"

St. Peter calmly replies, "Those are the lie clocks. Every single person on Earth has a lie clock. Each time someone tells a lie, the hands on his or her clock move."

"Oh," says the Newfie. He points to one of the clocks and says, "Who owns that clock there?"

"That one belongs to Mother Teresa. The hands have never moved, indicating that she has never told a lie."

"Incredible," says the Newfie. He points to another clock. "And who owns that clock there?"

St. Peter responds, "That clock belongs to Danny Williams. The hands have moved twice; that lets us know that Danny has only told two lies in his entire life."

"Where's Stephen Harper's clock?" asks the Newfie.

St. Peter lowers his head in disgust. "Stephen Harper's clock is in God's office. He's been using it as a ceiling fan for the past four years."

A new minister is visiting the homes of his congregation in Hawke's Bay. At one of the houses, it seems obvious to him there is someone at home, even though no one is answering the door. He can hear the radio playing and see the car in driveway, but still no one answers after repeated knocks. The minister wants to make sure the family knows he tried to visit them, so he takes out one of his business cards, writes "Revelation 3:20" on the back of it and sticks it in the door.

After the service the following Sunday, the minister is sitting in his office counting the offerings from the collection plates. He finds his business card has been returned in one of the plates. On the back reads another Bible reference added after his own: "Genesis 3:10."

Reaching for his Bible to check out the verse, he starts to laugh out loud once he gets to the right page. Revelation 3:20 starts with "Behold, I stand at the door and knock." Genesis 3:10 reads, "I heard your voice in the garden and I was afraid for I was naked."

One day, a Newfie dies, and instead of going up to heaven, he ends up going to hell. When he arrives, one of the devil's minions greets him and says, "Hey, buddy, I hope you like the heat because it gets mighty hot down here."

The Newfie says, "Sure t'ing, b'y. The weather in Newfoundland is always so bad that it'll be nice to get a bit of heat for a change." And with that, the Newfie starts to walk around and take in his new surroundings; he apparently has no issue with the heat.

The devil gets wind of what's going on, and he decides that because this is hell, he can't bear to have a happy Newfie wandering around making the devil look bad. He turns the up the heat, figuring the Newfie won't be able handle it.

After the heat is raised, the devil himself is sweating, so he goes to find the Newfie. He searches high and low. Eventually, he finds the Newfie standing in front of an open fire, making a cup of tea, singing "I'se The B'y."

"Newfie! Come over here!" the devil shouts. "I have more than doubled the temperature in hell, and you look like you're having a great time. How can you stand the heat?"

The Newfie replies, "Yes, b'y, 'tis wonderful grand here. This last winter on the island was so long that I don't think we got to see the sun for more than 20 minutes at a time. I didn't have enough wood stowed away to last, and I nearly froze to death at least twice. This heat is like having a vacation in Florida!"

The Newfie's response makes the devil angry. People in hell shouldn't be enjoying themselves. But the devil doesn't give up. He figures that if the Newfie loves the heat, he will surely hate the cold. Having hell freeze over is sure to be a way to make the stubborn Newfie unhappy.

The devil drops the temperature in hell. He makes it colder than it has ever been in Newfoundland. Confident the Newfie will be unhappy, the devil goes looking for him to enjoy the Newfie's misery. He spies the Newfie dancing on top of a huge snow-drift. The Newfie is shouting, "The Leafs won the playoffs! The Leafs won the playoffs!"

A British scholar decides to write a book about famous churches around the world. For his first chapter, he chooses to write about churches in Canada. He buys a plane ticket and flies to Vancouver. The scholar figures he'll start in Western Canada and work his way to the East Coast.

He goes inside the first church on his list and sees a golden telephone with a sign beside it that reads "$10,000 per call." The scholar is curious so he asks what the telephone is for.

The priest explains it's a direct line to heaven, and for $10,000, you can talk to God.

The British scholar thanks the priest and goes to the next church on his list, which is in Calgary. In this church, he sees the same golden telephone with the same sign beside it. The scholar figures the phone can't be used for the same purpose as the one in Vancouver, so he asks a nun what they use it for.

The nun tells him it's a direct line to heaven, and for $10,000, he can talk to God.

The British scholar thanks the nun and travels to churches in Edmonton, Regina, Winnipeg, Toronto, Ottawa, Montreal and Halifax, and at every church he visits, he sees the same golden telephone with the same "$10,000 per call" sign beside it. At each church, he asks what the phone is used for, and every time he gets the same answer.

The British scholar finally arrives in St. John's, and again he sees the golden telephone, but this time the sign beside it reads "$0.25 per call."

The scholar is intrigued, and while he's chatting with the church's minister, says, "Father, I have been in churches from Vancouver to Halifax, and each church contains the same telephone as yours. But in all the other churches in all the other provinces, the cost to call heaven is $10,000. Why is it so cheap here?"

The minister smiles and answers, "My son, you is in Newfoundland now. From here, 'tis a local call."

One afternoon, little Johnny is playing outdoors. Earlier in the day, he had taken his mother's broom from the closet to use as a horse, and he is now having a wonderful time. When it starts to get dark outside, Johnny's mother calls him in for the night, "Johnny, git yer arse in here! It's time for supper."

Reluctantly, Johnny goes inside, but he leaves the broom on the back porch. After supper, his mother can't find her broom, and when she asks Johnny if he has seen it, Johnny calls out from upstairs, "Mudder, I left the broom on the porch."

"Well," says his mother, "please go out and bring it in here, me son."

Johnny comes downstairs and tells his mother he's afraid of the dark and is too scared to get the broom from the porch.

His mother quietly says, "Johnny, my boy, Jesus lives on that porch, so there's nuthin' to be afraid of, is there?"

Johnny carefully pokes his head around the back door and calls out into the dark, "Jesus, my mudder says you lives on the back porch. Can you trow along that there broom?"

A young Newfie girl goes to a Catholic school that is run by a local group of nuns.

One day a sister walks up to the girl and asks her what she wants to be when she grows up.

The girl quickly replies, "A prostitute."

The nun grasps her chest and faints. The girl is kind enough to help the nun up from the floor. As soon as she's able, the nun asks the girl to repeat what she wants to be when she grows up.

"A prostitute," the girl answers again.

The nun grins and responds, "Thanks be to Jesus. I thought you said you wanted to be a Protestant."

An old Newfie has just died and is on his way to heaven. When he gets to St. Peter's Pearly Gates, he is met by an angel. The angel tells the Newfie he needs to answer one question before he can enter. The Newfie must tell the angel what God's name is.

"Oh, sure, me dear, dat's an easy one," the Newfie replies. "Sure as I'm standing here, God's name is Andy."

"What makes you think his name is Andy?" the surprised angel asks.

"Well," says the Newfie, "every Sunday we used to walk past the Salvation Army on our way to go trouting, and they always sang this song, 'Andy walks with me, Andy talks with me.'"

A Newfie minister tells his congregation, "Next week I'm plannin' to preach about the awful sin of lying. You all needs to read Mark, Chapter 17, to go along with what I'm gonna say."

The following Sunday, as he prepares to give his sermon, the minister asks for a show of hands to see how many have read Mark, Chapter 17. Every hand in the church goes up. The minister smiles and says, "Ha! Mark has only 16 chapters. Nobody here read a single word. Pretty sure there's much that we can all learn about lying."

There's a church in St. John's that's still being worked on, years after construction was first started on it. The workers have installed a "cage elevator" inside so they can move stuff up and down and to and from the upper and lower floors. As everyone soon finds out, the gate of elevator has to be closed or else the cage won't move from one floor to another.

One day, a worker, Peter, takes the elevator to the top floor, gets out and forgets to close the gate. Another worker on the first floor needs the elevator, but he can't call it down because the gate is open.

He calls out for the b'ys at the top to close the gate, but no one pays any attention to him. The worker decides that maybe the priest can help get Peter's attention to send down the elevator.

The worker finds the priest and drags him out into the yard of the church. He whispers in the priest's ear. After a few minutes the priest decides the only way to get Peter's attention is to let him know who is yelling.

The priest stands beside the church, looks up and calls out, "Peter! This is Father Smith. Close the gates!"

A Newfie appears before St. Peter at heaven's gates.

St. Peter starts to question the Newfie on the good things he did while alive. "Have you ever done anything of particular merit, something that shows how good of a person you are?" St. Peter asks.

"Well now, sir, one thing comes right to my mind," the Newfie says. "I came upon a gang of macho Torontonian thugs who were threatening a woman and her son. I yelled at them buggers to leave her alone, but by God they wouldn't listen to a word I says. So I walked right up to the biggest, meanest, ugliest one out of the lot. I gave him a clout over the head that rattled his brain, tripped him up and told him that if he didn't leave her alone, it was gonna be me that he would have to deal with."

St. Peter is really interested in the story. "When did this happen? I should have heard about this heroic act before now."

The Newfie looks down at his watch and answers, "B'y, dat was just a couple of minutes ago..."

A Pentecostal preacher from Petty Harbour finishes his sermon for the day and proceeds toward the back of the church for his usual greeting and handshaking as everyone leaves the church. After shaking a few adult hands he comes upon the seven-year-old son of one of the long-standing members of the church.

"Good morning, Freddy," the preacher says as he reaches out to shake Freddy's hand.

As the preacher takes Freddy's hand, he feels something in his palm. "What's this?" the preacher asks.

"Money," says Freddy with a big smile on his face. "It's for you!"

"I can't take your money, Freddy. It wouldn't be right," the preacher says.

"But I wants you to have it," says Freddy. After a short pause he continues, "My fadder says you is the poorest preacher we ever had, and I wants to help you."

A big, burly fisherman visits the local pastor's home and asks to see his wife. Even though the minister and his wife have not been in the town long, she is already a woman well known for her charity toward those less fortunate.

"My dear," the fisherman says in a broken voice, "I needs to make you aware of a terrible situation of a poor family that lives around here. The fadder died a year ago, the mudder is too sick to work and the nine children is starving to death. In two days they are going to be turned out into the cold unless some generous soul pays their rent. Sure only $400 will save the lot of them."

"How terrible!" exclaims the pastor's wife. "May I ask who you are?"

The fisherman blows his nose into his handkerchief. "I'm their landlord," he sobs.

A bayman recovering up from his wild Saturday night is sitting through what he feels is the longest Sunday sermon ever. He finds the service boring, and because he's still feeling hung over and tired, he nods off.

The priest has been watching the bayman the whole time. It's obvious he's not paying attention, and the priest is disgusted with the sight of the bayman sleeping in the back of the church. At the end of the sermon, the priest decides to make an example of the bayman.

He says to everyone in the church, "All those wishing to have a place in heaven, please stand."

Everyone in the room stands up except for the bayman sleeping in the back row.

Then the priest says loudly, "And all those wishing they could find a place in hell, please STAND UP!"

The hung-over bayman, catching only the last part of the sentence, groggily stands up while everyone else in the church sits down.

Confused and embarrassed, he says, "Fadder, I got no clue what we is voting on here, but it sure seems like you and me are the only ones standing for it!"

A nine-year-old girl is sitting beside her mother in the Basilica in St. John's when she starts feeling ill.

"Mommy," she says, "can we leave now?"

"No," her mother whispers.

"Well, I think I have to throw up!" the little girl says loud enough so that others hear.

"Then go out the front door and around to the back of the church and throw up behind one of them bushes that we planted last summer," says the mother.

In about two minutes, the little girl returns to her seat.

"Did you throw up?" her mother asks. "Do you feel better now, my dear?"

"Yes," the little girl replies.

"Well, that's good, but how could you have gone all the way 'round to the back of the church and return so quickly?"

"I didn't have to go out of the church, mommy," the little girl replies. "I just used the box out front that says 'For the sick.'"

A Newfie is coming out of the Salvation Army church. The officer is standing at the door, as he always is, to shake hands with the Sunday parishioners. He grabs the Newfie by the hand and pulls him aside.

The officer says to him, "My son, you needs to join the Army of the Lord!"

The man quickly replies, "I'm already in the Army of the Lord, officer."

"Well then, how come I only sees you at Christmas and Easter?" asks the officer.

The man whispers back, "My God, I'm in the secret service. Don't tell anyone I was here."

A Newfie man and his wife attend a small service at the local church. The man is moved by the sermon, so he stops to shake the reverend's hand after the service.

The Newfie says, "Reverend, that was the best damn sermon I ever heard in this church!"

The reverend replies, "Oh! Why, thank you, me son, but please don't you start swearing in the house of the Lord."

"I'm sorry, Reverend, but I can't help meself. 'Twas such a damn good sermon!"

The reverend replies, "Please, b'y. You can't come in 'ere swearing where other people is at!"

"Okay, Reverend, but I needs you to know that I figured it was so goddamn good that I put $5000 in the collection plate."

The reverend's eyes open wide as he remarks, "No shit, b'y!"

Three Newfie fishermen find themselves at the Pearly Gates at the same time. St. Peter eyes all three of them and decides that a small skill-testing question might be in order. He's pretty sure these guys never stepped through the doors of a church in their lives.

He calls the first one forward and asks, "What is Easter?"

The fisherman thinks for a second and answers, "Easter is dat day off in the fall just around moose-huntin' season. It's when we eats lots of turkey, watches TV and give thanks for all of God's goodness."

"I'm sorry, that's wrong," says St. Peter, and the guy vanishes down through the clouds with a puff of smoke. St. Peter turns to the next fisherman and asks him the same question.

"B'y, dat's an easy one," he says. "Easter is a holiday that celebrates Christ. What happens during Easter is dis here: we all exchanges gifts because them wise b'ys gave stuff to the baby Jesus. Now den, depending on where you lives, you might decorate a tree and string lights up around."

"That's enough!" shouts St. Peter, and the second fisherman disappears down through the clouds. There is only one Newfie left, and St. Peter turns to him and asks the same question.

The last fisherman swallows hard and begins. "Easter is the holiest event on the Christian calendar, occurring each year around the time of Jewish Passover. It celebrates the events of the last days of Jesus' life when he was betrayed by one of his disciples and turned over to the Romans. The Romans crucified him, hanging him on a cross with nails through his hands and feet. He was stabbed in the side and made to wear a crown of thorns. He was buried in a nearby cave that was sealed with a large boulder."

A broad smile of delight begins to creep across St. Peter's face. "Please continue," he suggests, happy that at least one of the fisherman has paid attention.

The third fisherman continues, "Every year dat big rock der is rolled away so Jesus can come out for a while and…uh…uh…and if he sees his shadow den we gots six more long weeks of winter."

A drunken Newfie staggers into a Catholic church in Edmonton, sits down in a confession box and says nothing. The priest inside waits for a few minutes, but the man doesn't make a sound. The bewildered priest coughs to attract the Newfie's attention, but still he says nothing. The priest then knocks on the wall three times in a final attempt to get the man to speak.

Finally, the drunk replies, "Don't bodder knocking here buddy, there ain't no paper in this one, either."

A young man from Botwood asks his father to use the car. The father replies, "Look here, you're not usin' that car unless you cuts your hair off."

The young man replies, "But fadder, Jesus had long hair! Nobody ever told Jesus to cut his hair." His father says, "Yes b'y, but Jesus walked everywhere, didn't he?"

Cathy, a middle-aged housewife from St. John's, has a heart attack and ends up at the Health Sciences Centre. She is quickly rushed into surgery, and the doctors have to operate for more than six hours to save her.

Halfway through the surgery, Cathy almost dies. She starts walking toward the light, and she meets God.

Boldly, she asks, "God, is this the end for me? Have I come to meet my maker?"

God quickly answers, "No, Cathy, you still have 30 or 40 years left yet. It will be a long while before we meet again."

Cathy recovers quickly and decides that if she is going to live another 30 years, she needs to do something about how she looks. She stays in the hospital and convinces her husband to pay for a facelift, liposuction, breast implants and a tummy tuck. Before leaving the hospital, Cathy even has someone come in and change her hair colour and do her makeup—by all accounts she is a new woman. She looks half her age and feels great. When the doctors tell Cathy she's finally allowed to go home, she walks out the hospital and is killed by an ambulance speeding up to the hospital.

She arrives in front of God again, and asks, "God, it's me Cathy. The last time I saw you, you said I had another 30 to 40 years left!"

God squints his eyes and replies, "Sorry, Cathy, I didn't recognize you."

Two five-year-old Newfie boys are standing at the toilet to pee. One says, "Your thingy doesn't have any skin on it! It don't look like mine."

"I got circumcised," the other boy replies proudly. "That means they cut the skin off the end of it."

"How old were you when dey cut it off? Did dat hurt, den?" the first boy asks.

"Mudder says I was two days old," the second boy says. "You bet it hurt, I didn't walk for a year after dat!"

One Sunday night, an elderly couple from around the bay is watching a television preacher on TV. The preacher faces the camera and announces, "My friends, I'd like to share my healing powers with everyone watching this program. Place one hand on top of your TV and the other hand on the part of your body that ails you, and I will heal you through the power of Christ."

The old woman has been having terrible stomach problems, so she places one hand on the television and her other hand on her stomach. Meanwhile, her husband approaches the television and places one hand on top of the TV and the other hand on his crotch.

With a frown his wife says, "Eddie, that man is going on about healing the sick, not raising the dead."

It's Boxing Day, and the minister of a small outport church notices the baby Jesus that was part of the nativity scene is missing. He starts to look around the church, but then notices a little boy outside, dragging a wagon through the snow. In the back is the missing baby Jesus.

He stops the boy and asks, "Where did you get the baby Jesus, my son?"

"From the church, fadder," the boy responds.

The minister asks, "But why did you take the baby Jesus from the manger?"

The boy answers, "Fadder, I prayed last Sunday for a new wagon. I told God that if I got one for Christmas, he could go for a ride in it."

A woman from Shea Heights decides to prepare her last will and testament and make her final requests. She tells her priest she has two final requests. First, she wants to be cremated, and second, she wants her ashes scattered all over George Street.

"Why George Street?" asks the priest.

"If I'm put to rest on George Street, then I'll know for sure that my husband visits me at least two times a week."

A nun is walking in the Basilica in St. John's when one of the priests notices she's put on a little weight.

"Gaining a little weight, are we Sister Susan?" he asks.

"No, Father. It's just a little gas left over from the pea soup we had last night," Sister Susan explains.

About a month later the priest notices Sister Susan has gained even more weight. "Gaining some weight, are we Sister Susan?" he asks again.

"Oh no, Father. Just a little gas left over from the baked beans we had for lunch," she replies.

A couple months later the priest notices Sister Susan pushing a baby carriage along the sidewalk in front of the church.

He leans over, looks in the carriage and says, "Cute little fart you've got there, Sister."

A preacher retires and moves around the bay to enjoy life and practice his gardening hobby. Soon after moving in he realizes he needs a lawn mower, or else the grass on his lawn is going to get out of hand. The preacher heads into Deer Lake to buy his lawn mower, and on the way he sees a sign by the side of the highway advertising a lawn mower for sale. He stops at the house, and a teenager comes out to greet him. The preacher asks about the lawn mower, and the teen says it's behind the house. The two go around to look at the lawn mower. The engine sputters along, but the preacher increases the speed of the engine and mows a few strips of lawn. Satisfied, he settles on a price of $25.

Later that day, the teenager is riding his bicycle when he spies the preacher pulling on the engine-starter rope. The boy stops and watches for a couple minutes.

He asks, "What's wrong?"

"I can't get this mower started. Do you know how?"

The teen says, "Yep."

"Well, how do you do it? Tell me!" the preacher yells.

The boy replies, "You have to swear at it something fierce."

The preacher looks at the teenager. "Now, you listen here. I'm a preacher, and if I ever did cuss, not saying I have, I've forgotten how to do it after all these years."

With a wise smile on his face, the teen says, "Preacher, you keep on pulling that rope and believe me, it'll all come back to ya."

A Newfie priest is driving to St. John's and gets stopped for speeding on the Trans Canada Highway. The RCMP officer smells alcohol on the priest's breath and notices an empty wine bottle on the floor of the car.

The officer says, "Sir, have you been drinking?"

"Just water, my son," says the priest.

The officer replies, "Then why can I smell wine all the way out here?"

The priest glances at the bottle, looks at the officer and says, "Praise be to Jesus! He's done it again!"

Three young boys are playing outside. One boy is Irish, one boy is French and the third boy is a Newfie, but all three of them are good Catholic b'ys.

The French boy announces, "My uncle is a priest, and everyone calls him Father."

The Irish boy says, "Well, my uncle is a cardinal, and everyone calls him Your Eminence."

The Newfie boy scoffs. "Sure, dat's nuthin'. My uncle weighs 350 pounds. When people sees him, they always says 'My God.'"

One weekend, Bob goes to church in Corner Brook, and sits and listens to the minister give a wonderful sermon. Eventually, the minister calls out that anyone wishing to pray can come forward and kneel at the altar. Bob stands up, makes his way to the front of the church and kneels before the minister.

The minister asks Bob what he wants to pray for.

Bob looks up into the face of the minister and says, "I needs to pray for my hearing, please."

The minister prays with Bob and asks God to help with Bob's hearing. After a few minutes the minister looks at Bob and says, "How is your hearing now, Bob?"

Bob responds, "I'll let you know next week; my hearing isn't until Thursday."

A Newfie and a Torontonian end up in heaven at the same time. While waiting to get in, the man from Toronto starts talking about how he ended up at St. Peter's gates.

The Newfie quietly says he froze to death before the Torontonian launches into telling his story.

"Well, I thought my wife was having an affair. Even though she denied it, I made it my goal to catch her in the act. I hired a private investigator; he found nothing. I did a background check on everyone she knew; I found nothing. I had her followed for days at a time, and still I found nothing. But one evening I came home and saw a strange car in the driveway. I raced inside and searched every room in the house. When I didn't find anyone, I got so excited that she was telling the truth I had a heart attack and died."

The Newfie looks at him sheepishly and says, "Too bad you didn't bother checking the freezer."

On his latest visit to Newfoundland, the pope decides it's time to try something new. Travelling to the airport in Deer Lake, the pope asks to drive the limo. The driver, being a good Catholic, feels he can't refuse the Holy Father, so he stops the car and the pope takes the wheel and starts down the highway. The pope hasn't driven a car in years, so he pushes the gas pedal too hard and is soon going over the speed limit. Eventually, the flashing lights of a police car slow him down, and the pope pulls over to the side of the road.

The police officer comes up to the window and is darn near floored by the sight of the pope behind the wheel. The officer stammers, "I'll be back in a moment, your Holiness." He calls into the station and asks to speak to the chief of police. The flustered policeman asks what he should do.

The chief says, "Who'd you pull over?"

"Someone really important," replies the officer.

"The premier?" the chief asks.

"No," the officer says. "I says REALLY important."

"The prime minister?" questions the chief.

The officer answers, "No, REALLY, REALLY important."

"Who the heck did you pull over?" the chief yells.

"Well, sir, I don't rightly know who he is, but the pope's his chauffer."

A Newfie is walking along the beach in Nova Scotia, deep in prayer. When he finishes praying, he looks up to heaven and says, "God b'y, I knows you out there. Please grant me just one wish."

Suddenly, the Newfie hears a loud voice that says, "My son, because you believe in me, I'll grant you one wish."

"All right then, buddy," the Newfie says, "Build me a bridge that goes from here to Newfoundland. Then I can drive there whenever I wants to."

God is silent for a few minutes and then replies, "My son, while what you have asked for is noble, it is not something even I can do. Think about the engineering that is needed to build a bridge like that. I can build the bridge, but I can't justify such a use of power. Take some more time and think of a wish that will help your fellow man."

The Newfie stops and thinks. After a few minutes he says, "Okay then, God. I have been married three times and divorced twice. Each time I end up divorced, my ex-wife says I have no idea what a woman wants. I wish I knew what it will take to make my third wife happy. Please tell me what a woman really wants."

God answers, "Do you want one lane or two on that bridge?"

One quiet afternoon, Father Abbott is sitting in his office at the parish church in Fortune. He answers a phone call from Revenue Canada. The official on the other end of the line asks stiffly, "Father, I need to confirm some information for the Government of Canada. You must tell the truth. Do you have a parishioner named Garge Smith?"

"That I do," answers the priest honestly.

"I need to confirm that he is a member of your congregation," says the official.

The priest replies, "That he is."

"Well, sir," says the voice on the phone, "did he donate $10,000 to the church this year? And remember, you must tell the truth."

"That he will," states the priest.

Jimmie, an elderly Newfie, wanders into a confessional and sits down. The priest waits for Jimmie to start, but he doesn't say a word. After a few minutes, the priest asks Jimmie what he needs to confess.

Jimmie replies slowly, "My boy, I's 92 years old. I got a wife, and we been married for 70 years on Saturday."

The priest quickly offers his congratulations.

"Now hold on a minute," Jimmie says. "That's not all I gots to say. Last week I picked up two university girls, and we got ourselves a motel room. An' I had the best sex of my life."

The priest, surprised at the old man's admission, asks quietly, "Do you repent for your sins, my child?"

The old Newfie looks through the screen and says, "What sins are you talkin' 'bout?"

Shocked that the Newfie doesn't know he's done wrong, the priest accuses, "What kind of Catholic are you?"

Jimmie says, "Cat'lic? I'm not Cat'lic."

The priest asks, "Then why are you confessing to me?"

"Confessin'?" Jimmie laughs. "I'm tellin' every-one I can find!"

Two Pentecostal brothers who are known for get-ting into trouble are sent to the pastor for discipline. The boys' parents think the pastor can scare the boys into being good.

The pastor looks at one of the boys and says, "Where is God?"

Neither of the boys makes a sound.

The pastor yells at the other boy, "I says, WHERE IS GOD?"

Both boys jump out of their chairs, run out of the church and hurry home. They get into the house, slam the door and are still out of breath when their mother asks what's wrong.

The first boy says, "Mudder, I t'inks we're in lots of trouble this time. It looks like God is missing."

The second boy looks up and says, "Yup, and the pastor t'inks we did it."

On Fridays, a lone Salvationist in a Catholic out-port community grills steaks while the Catholics eat fish. This has happened every Friday for years, and every Friday, the Catholics can fair taste the forbidden steaks as their neighbour grills them to his heart's content.

The Catholics work on the Salvationist, trying their hardest to convert him to Catholicism—they don't want to smell the delicious steak on Fridays anymore. Finally, the Salvationist gives in.

He's taken to the local priest who sprinkles him with holy water and chants, "Born a Salvationist, raised a Salvationist, now a Catholic."

The Catholics are on cloud nine. They figure their Fridays of smelling the delicious steaks are over, but it doesn't take long before they start smelling grilled beef on Fridays again. The Catholics run to the ex-Salvationist's house to remind him he can only eat fish on Fridays, no steak. To their surprise, they find the man standing over his barbecue, sprinkling holy water on his steak saying, "Born a cow, raised a cow, now a fish!"

St. Peter is standing at the gates to heaven when three Newfies and their wives line up waiting to get in. St. Peter is in a foul mood, so he's making it quite hard to enter heaven.

The first Newfie owned a bar when he was alive, and St. Peter says, "Today you are not welcome in heaven. You drank too much and sold liquor to those who beat their wives and children when they were drunk. You even married a woman named after the drink—Sherry. Be gone."

The next couple walks up. St. Peter looks them up and down and says, "You, sir, are a banker. You spent your whole life making money. You loved money more than you loved God. You even married a woman called Penny. You have no right to enter heaven."

The third Newfie looks at his wife and says, "We better go, Fanny. Der's no hope for us here."

One Sunday, a minister in a small outport Anglican church preaches about the importance of forgiveness and how to live your life without making enemies. He ends his sermon by asking if there is anyone who can say they truly have no enemies.

The church is silent for several minutes. No one utters a word. Then an elderly lady raises her hand.

The minister says to the woman, "Please come forward and tell everyone how you know you have no enemies."

The old woman slowly shuffles to the front of the church. It takes her quite a few minutes; everyone waits to hear her answer. She finally reaches the altar and turns to face the congregation made up of her friends and neighbours. The minister asks again for her to explain how she has managed to live her life without making enemies.

Q: How can you tell which people in heaven are Newfies?

A: They're the ones who all want to go home.

She answers, "They all is dead!"

An American, a Scot and a Newfie are in an airplane accident and none of them survives. All three end up in the same hospital, and just as the American is being wheeled to the morgue, he sits up and scares the bejesus out of the nurses and the doctor. They ask him how he came back to life.

He tells them how the three men were trying to get into heaven, but St. Peter decided they were all too young to die. St. Peter told the men that if they gave a donation of $50 he would send them back to Earth.

The American handed over $50 to St. Peter and back to Earth he was sent.

The doctor asks what happened to the other two men.

The American says, "Well, sir, the last thing I remember is that the Scot was trying to get a lower price, and the Newfie was waiting for the government to pay his bill."

It's a beautiful Sunday morning in outport Newfoundland. All the good parishioners are sitting in church, dutifully listening to the preacher speak his sermon. The devil is sitting in hell, watching the church service, and decides he needs to pay everyone in the church a visit.

Suddenly, the church doors burst open with a bang. Rolling, black clouds fill the church, and the devil walks through the aisles, leaving fire and brimstone in his wake. Almost everyone jumps out of the pews and runs away screaming. The only two people left are the minister and an elderly fisherman.

Satan is completely confused by the reaction of the churchgoers; he expected them to have enough faith to face him. He has watched them show up to church for years, and from what he can tell, they believe in God and are extremely devout. He points to the minister and says, "You, man of God! I can see why you didn't turn from your faith and run away from me. You are standing in the house of your Lord; every day you preach against me and my wickedness and you aren't afraid of me."

"But YOU," the devil says to the elderly fisherman. "Why are you still standing before me? Is your faith so strong that you think you can stand up to me? You should have run away, old man."

The fisherman slowly crosses one leg over the other and looks the devil straight in the eye. "Look here, buddy. I can't believe you don't know who I is. Don't you remember my face? Lordy jumpin' dyin', I been married to your sister for 40 years now!"

CHAPTER SEVEN

Newfies on The Rock

No matter where Newfies live, they are never more at home than on the island. And when Newfies feel at home, their guard is down, and they end up creating the best stories and finding the funniest jokes. Nothing makes a more perfect breeding ground for all the silliness that makes its way west than Newfies on The Rock...

A plane is coming in to land in St. John's and the fog is so thick the captain can't see anything. The pilot realizes he will have to use his skill alone to land the plane. He takes a deep breath, looks at his Newfie co-pilot and starts checking off the things they need to do before landing. He calls to the co-pilot: flaps, check; landing gear, check. After a few tense minutes, they manage to get the plane on the ground but have to slam on the brakes as soon as the wheels touch down. They come to a screeching halt just short of the edge of the runway.

The pilot exclaims, "Goodness, that must be the shortest runway I have ever seen!"

The Newfie co-pilot stands up in the cockpit, looks to the left of the plane and then to the right. He says, "Jumpin' dyin! It's about the widest, too!"

Sally's husband John passes away, and to complete the funeral arrangements, she makes a trip across the barrens to the *Compass* office to put a notice in the paper. The receptionist offers her sympathies and asks what Sally wants the notice to say.

Sally says, "Just write 'John died.'"

The receptionist stares at Sally and responds, "That's it? Don't you want to say more? If 'tis dollars you're worried about, you gets five free words."

"Fine," Sally says, and she thinks for a minute. "I wants, 'John died. Quad for sale.'"

Little Johnny is looking at an old photo album, and he points to a faded snapshot of a young man. He asks his mother, "Who's this feller layin' on the beach beside you?" Little Johnny stares at the young, muscular man with curly brown hair.

The boy's mother's face lights up at the memory, and she says, "That's your father, Johnny."

Johnny scoffs, "If he's me dad, who's the bald fat man living with us now?"

On the first day of Grade 4, Jimmy's teacher asks everyone to count to 100. Most of the students do really well. One of them gets to 56 without any mistakes, and Jimmy is overjoyed to later tell his father that he managed to count all the way to 100 with only two mistakes.

Jimmy's father says, "You did so good because you're from Newfoundland, me son."

The next day during language class, the teacher asks everyone to say the alphabet. Jimmy does really well again, and he is happy to tell his father he only missed the letter *N*.

Jimmy's father says again, "You did so good because you're from Newfoundland, me son." The next day during gym class, Jimmy notices he's a lot bigger than the other boys. He can jump higher and run faster than all of them.

When he gets home, he asks his father about this. Jimmy says, "Dad, am I bigger than all of the boys because I'm from Newfoundland?"

Jimmy's father shakes his head and says, "No, me son, you're bigger than all the rest because you're 16."

In a court of law, a judge looks down at a Newfie woman and asks, "After you put the poison in the Jiggs dinner and served it to your husband, did you ever feel any remorse for what you had done?"

"Yes," says the woman. "As soon as he asked for seconds."

Two Newfies, Jenny and Joan, are standing in front of the stove boiling up some corn on the cob to go with supper.

Jenny says to Joan, "Can you pass me some tongs, please?"

Joan looks at Jenny and responds, "Is you makin' fun of me?"

Jenny looks stunned and says, "Wha's up with you? I'm lookin' for tongs to take the corn out of the pot. Das all, maid."

Joan laughs. "Oh my God! I always thought they was called thongs!"

A man walks into a pet shop in St. John's. He wants to buy a parrot.

The owner points to three parrots sitting on a perch and says, "Buddy, the first parrot there is $500."

The customer says, "Jeez, b'y, that's a lot. How come it costs so much?"

The owner replies, "Oh, that parrot can drive a speedboat."

The man thinks that's a pretty impressive feat.

The owner pipes up and says, "The parrot sittin' alongside him is $1000."

The customer asks, "Well, den, what's he do for $1000?"

The owner replies, "Well, my son, he can drive the boat and navigate by the stars."

The man is further impressed with the second bird and says, "Well, den, how much is that last bird?"

"That last bird costs $2000," the owner replies.

The customer is shocked by the price difference, "My God, what can dat bird do dat's worth dat much money?"

The owner says, "Buddy, I don't rightly know. I haven't seen him do a thing since he got here, but all the other birds calls him Captain."

Did You Hear...

About the Newfie woman who was pretty sure her husband was cheating on her? None of her children looked like him.

About the Newfie who set out to become the best ice-fisherman on the island? He went out one day and caught 500 pounds of ice. The trouble started when his wife tried to cook it all at once and drowned.

About the first Newfie to win an Olympic gold medal? His parents were so proud they had it bronzed.

About the two Newfies who froze to death at the drive-in movie theatre? They went to see "Closed for the Season."

About the Newfie who was overjoyed at finishing his jigsaw puzzle in just three months? On the box it specified five-to-eight years.

A bum approaches a well-dressed Newfie on the street outside of Atlantic Place in St. John's.

BUM: "Hey buddy, spare a few dollars?"

NEWFIE: "Is you gonna spend it to go huntin'?"

BUM: "I don't hunt, sir."

NEWFIE: "Well den, fishin', I s'pose?"

BUM: "No fishin' either."

NEWFIE: "Waste it on booze?"

BUM: "I'm hungry. I'm looking for a meal."

NEWFIE: "Den come on. The missus is cookin' up a big scoff at home."

The bum accepts, but eventually has to ask, "Why are you bringing me home? Won't your missus be mad?"

The Newfie says, "Probably, but I wants her to see what happens when a man don't fish, hunt or drink."

Marg is lying on her deathbed and calls her husband to her side.

"Harv," she says, "You is only a young man. I knows you'll marry again."

Harv looks down at his wife and replies, "Marg, you knows you're my one true love. Sure I couldn't love anyone else."

Marg says, "I knows dat it's gonna happen. Just promise me one t'ing."

"What's dat?" asks Harv.

"For the love of God, don't let her wear my good Sunday clothes," says Marg.

"Lard Jesus, Marg, you don't have to worry der. Yer Sunday best is too big for Effie."

A Newfie is driving along and has to slam on the brakes. When he looks up he realizes he almost ran over a three-legged chicken. He gets out of his truck and tries to run after the chicken, but he can't catch it. He finally gives up trying and just follows the chicken down the road. Eventually, it leads him to a house and skitters into the backyard.

The Newfie knocks on the front door and yells out that he wants to speak to the man who raises three-legged chickens. The owner opens the door, and the Newfie tells the man he's amazed chickens with three legs exist.

Q: Why did the Newfies riding in the back of a truck drown when it went through the ice?

A: They couldn't get the tailgate down.

The man looks at the Newfie and says, "Yes, b'y, I growed 'em like that cause my favourite part of the chicken is the drumsticks."

The Newfie is curious and asks, "Well then, what's three-legged chicken taste like?"

The man laughs. "I dunno, buddy, they is awful hard to catch."

You Might Be a
Newfie Computer Geek if...

✔ Your email address ends in "@lukiesboat. nl.ca."

✔ You've used a CD as a beer coaster when company is over.

✔ Your computer is worth more than your wife's car.

✔ Your screen saver is a picture of your boat, your quad or your Ski-Doo.

✔ You've used your CD burner as a beer-can holder.

✔ Your home page is www.downhomelife. com.

There Once Was a Bayman Who Was Able to Prove He Was Smarter than Everyone He Knew...

He sold his TV set to buy a VCR. "You gots to keep up with dem Joneses, me son."

He sent away to the Eaton's catalogue for a new wife—he liked her snap on page 53.

When Newfoundland moved to the metric system (Fahrenheit to Celsius), he went to work telling everyone how hot it was. He argued up and down that it was 90° C.

He boasted to the b'ys that his car went faster after he put in the new starting motor.

He was speeding through the straight when he got pulled over by the RCMP. When the officer asked him if he knew why he got stopped, the man told the officer that it must be because of his bald tires.

One night when it was blowing a gale, he tied his car to the fence post so it wouldn't blow away.

Driving home from town one evening, he noticed he was low on gas. He drove as fast as the car would go so he could get home before the car was on empty.

A Newfie goes down to the wharf and asks the captain of a fishing boat if he has any work available.

The captain gives the Newfie a huge application form and tells him to fill it out and bring it back. The Newfie goes home, fills out the paperwork and returns it to the captain. He goes through the Newfie's application with a fine-tooth comb and after three days decides to give the Newfie a try. On the second day the Newfie is aboard the boat, a foreigner walks onto the deck and asks for a job. The captain hires him on the spot.

The Newfie is put out by the fact that the foreigner didn't have to fill out the same application form, so he asks the captain about it. The captain tells the Newfie it's because the foreigner has an honest face.

The Newfie accepts his answer, and later when the two new employees are cleaning the deck, a huge wave comes along and sweeps the foreigner off the deck along with the bucket and mop he was using. The Newfie walks up to the captain and says smugly, "You know that foreigner you hired that you says looks honest? Well, he just took off with your bucket and mop."

A small outport community acquires a young new teacher for their one-room school, and two boys are arguing over which one the teacher likes more. Each boy is sure he's the favourite student.

When they get their math tests back, one of the boys is able to confirm that the teacher likes him the most. He says to the other boy, "I told you miss likes me better than she likes you. On me math test, I got kisses beside all of me sums!"

Two Newfies are driving home one night, both enjoying a bottle of Blue Star. They aren't causing any trouble, but when the car swerves going around a turn, they suddenly see police lights.

The passenger panics and yells, "My Jesus, buddy, we're screwed now!"

The driver looks at him and says, "Okay, do what I does, and don't you dare say a word."

The driver peels the label off his bottle of Blue Star and sticks it to his forehead while the cop steps out of his cruiser. The passenger does exactly the same thing just as the officer taps on the window.

The officer asks, "Have you boys been drinking tonight?"

The driver looks innocently at the cop and says, "My God, no sir, we're on the patch."

Quite the ladies man, Randy can never figure out why he doesn't impress the girls on the beach. He asks his lifeguard friend for some advice. The lifeguard seems to know the problem right off the bat.

"Stop wearing dem baggy trunks, luh. You needs to be in style for the ladies—like me. Go and git yerself a pair of them there Speedos—'bout two sizes too small, drop a potato down in dem and you'll get all the ladies you can handle."

Randy does as he is told, and the next weekend he sports his new bathing suit at the beach. The reaction of the ladies is a little less positive than Randy planned for, with most turning away laughing or looking slightly sick.

He finds his friend and tells him about the reaction. The lifeguard takes stock of Randy and his new garb and says, "You fool. The friggin' potato goes in the front."

A Newfie and a mainlander apply for a job at an oil-drilling firm based in St. John's. Both men have almost identical qualifications, so they are asked to complete a pre-employment test. Both men get 9 out of the 10 questions right. The manager lets the Newfie know he's giving the position to the mainlander.

The Newfie is right rotted with the decision. He says, "My God, b'y, what kind of place is dis? We're on The Rock, I'm from The Rock and we both got nine of dem questions right. Jeezus, b'y, I should get dat job."

The manager looks at the Newfie and replies, "We based our decision on the incorrect answer, not on your correct answers."

The Newfie asks, "Jumpin' holy Jeezus, how can one wrong answer be any different than another wrong answer?"

"That's easy," answers the manager. "On question number four, the mainlander's answer was 'I don't know.' You, my friend, put down 'Needer do I.'"

A policeman is sitting in his patrol car on George Street when he spies a Newfie stumble out of a bar, walk over to the parking lot, pull his keys out of his pocket and try to unlock five different cars before he manages to unlock his own.

The officer observes him turn the wipers on and off twice, honk the horn once and turn the lights on and off three times. He then sees the man back the car up a few inches and stop and wait for a carload of people to drive by. The man eventually pulls the car into the middle of the street, turns it off and does nothing.

The officer, after recording his notes, walks over to the Newfie, carrying a Breathalyzer. The policeman asks the Newfie to step outside the car because he needs to be tested before being allowed to drive. The Newfie complies, and to the officer's amazement, the Breathalyzer shows no alcohol in the Newfie's system. The officer tells the Newfie that he has to accompany him back to the police station because the Breathalyzer must be broken.

The Newfie looks at the officer and says, "I doubt it. Tonight I'm the designated decoy."

Overheard at Ches's Fish and Chips:

MAINLANDER: "Do you serve crabs?"

NEWFIE: "My dear, we serves anyone here."

Margaret and her husband have seven children, all of them girls and all of them over the age of 10. Margaret finds out she's pregnant with their eighth child, and she isn't happy about it.

Her husband, on the other hand, is awful proud to be having another child. He tells everyone he meets that he's sure this one is going be a boy.

When the baby is born, he has bright red hair, but Margaret and her husband have coal-black hair. Margaret's husband looks at her and says, "Jeezus, Margaret, what happened to his head?"

Shaking her head, Margaret replies, "After 10 years, rust, b'y, 'tis rust."

Every year, Fred and his wife Flossie watch an open-cockpit plane land near the pond in Blaketown. Fred has never been in a plane, and every year he asks Flossie if he can go for a ride. Every year the price is the same—$50—and Flossie always says, "That ride is $50. And $50 is $50," so Fred never goes for a ride.

This year, the pilot overhears their discussion, and he tells them if they can keep quiet for the whole ride, he won't charge them. They agree to not make a peep and climb into the plane.

The pilot does everything he can to make them scream. He does dips and rolls, but neither of them makes a sound. He's surprised, so he repeats the tricks again, but still no sound comes from the back of the plane.

When they land, the pilot says he's impressed with the couple because they didn't make any noise at all.

Fred finally speaks. "Well, when Flossie fell out, I was going to say something, but $50 is $50."

The Molson brewery in St. John's is famous for having the slackest employees in the company, so they hire a new manager from the mainland to take care of things. On his first day, he wants to make an impression of authority on the employees, so he walks up to the first guy he sees being lazy and asks, "How much do you make a week?"

Buddy responds, "I makes $300 a week."

The manager hands him $600 and says, "There's two weeks' pay. Don't come back." Buddy walks out without saying a word.

The manager turns to the other employees and asks, "What did that lazy fool do around here, anyway?"

Grinning hugely, one of the workers looks at the manager and answers, "He's the delivery guy from the pizza place down the street."

It's a foggy night, and Andy finds himself drunk and staggering down the road. He knows he isn't too far from town, but he doesn't know if he's gonna make it. While he's stumbling along, he comes upon a stopped car. The car is empty, and Andy is so tired he climbs into the passenger's seat for a rest. Suddenly the car starts to move slowly, and Andy gets to town after all. As the car coasts through town, Andy jumps out at the local bar.

He walks in and tells the unlikely story to the bartender. The bartender looks at him suspiciously and has to admit it's odd that the car rolled into town on its own, and every time the car went close to the ditch an arm came in the window and steered it back toward the road. In his drunken state, Andy decides it must have been the hand of God.

A few beers later, three guys walk in. They stop at the bar and stare at Andy. The biggest fella of the group walks over, picks Andy up by the shirt, turns to his friends and says, "And 'ere is the asshole that was sittin' in the front seat while we pushed the damn car home."

Brenda is busy making supper when she hears a knock at the front door. She hurries to see who is calling and opens it to find Tim, who works at the Molson plant with her husband Bill. She quickly asks Tim in and shuts the door behind him.

Tim tells Brenda to sit down because he has some news that might shock her.

Brenda is instantly worried and asks, "Tim, where's Bill at?"

Tim looks at her sadly and says, "Brenda, there was an accident at the plant. I'm sorry to be the one to tell ya, but your Bill drowned when he fell into a beer tank."

Brenda is shocked at the news and asks, "Well, Tim, did he at least go quickly?"

Tim has no choice but to tell Brenda the truth. "No, my dear. See, he got out three times to go pee."

Johnny was told his whole life how his father, grandfather and great-grandfather could all walk on water on their 19th birthdays. As the story went, on each of their birthdays, the men walked across the pond to the pub and had their first legal drink.

Q: How do you know that a Newfie invented the toothbrush?

A: Anyone else would have called it a teethbrush.

As Johnny's birthday nears, he is more than excited about being able to walk on water. He boasts to his friends that he is a little like Jesus. He tells everyone of his grand plan to walk on water on his birthday. One of his friends pulls him aside and reminds him, "B'y, you can't swim a'toll. Wha' happens if you sinks?"

Johnny jokes, "Go 'way wit'cha, b'y. Fadder did it, grandfadder did it, even me great-grandfadder walked over the water, so by God, so can I."

On his birthday, Johnny and his friend row out to the middle of the pond, and Johnny steps over the side of the boat. He sinks like a rock. His friend just manages to pull him back in the boat before he drowns.

Soaked to the skin and looking like a drowned rat, Johnny returns home to see his granny. Johnny asks why he couldn't walk on water.

His granny shakes her head and calmly replies, "Johnny, Johnny. Yer fadder, grandfadder and great-grandfadder was born in January. You was born in July."

In the middle of the night during a terrible rainstorm, Bruce is lying in his bed in Norman's Cove. All of a sudden he is woken up by a terrible knocking at the porch door. He stomps to the door and is faced with a soaking-wet drunk he has never laid eyes on before. The man asks him, "Sir, can you 'elp a feller out and give me a push?"

Bruce immediately replies, "Buddy, you're nuts if you thinks I'm getting soaked to help you." He slams the door in the drunk's face and walks back to the bedroom.

Bruce isn't even through the bedroom door when his wife lays into him about helping thy neighbour and following the Bible. She won't let it rest. Bruce gets tired of listening to her yap about the drunk guy, so he goes to find him.

Bruce pulls on a coat and opens the front door. It's black as sin outside. He can't see his hand in front of his face, so he calls out, "Hey, buddy, you still there?"

The drunk yells back, "Yes, I needs a push!"

Bruce calls out, "Where are you?"

The drunk yells, "On the swing!"

An RNC officer notices a car weave past him late on Friday night, so he immediately turns on his lights and pulls the car over. The officer walks up to the car window and shines his flashlight into the driver's face. The officer says, "Buddy, your eyes are awful fuzzy. Did you just come from George Street?"

"Yessss," the driver slurs, "but from 'ere your eyes are glazed. Did you just come from Tim Hortons?"

Buddy spent the night in the tank.

Martin is sitting on the bridge of his house when his wife clouts him over the head.

"Mary mother of God, what'd you do that for?" yelps Martin. His wife hands him a small slip of paper with the name Edith and the numbers 7492 scrawled on it.

Martin looks calmly at his wife and explains. "Now, my ducky, that's just the 'orse I bet on last week." Martin's wife eyes him suspiciously and walks away.

Two days later, his wife walks up and gives him an even bigger clout over the head.

Martin yells, "Jaysus, woman! What was dat fer?"

"Ha!" his wife says. "Your horse called. She didn't leave a message."

An Englishman and a Newfie are sitting in a pub on George Street. The Englishman is complaining about his arthritis, and the Newfie is complaining about his broken arm. The door opens, and a man walks in and takes a stool at the bar.

The Englishman looks at the man and exclaims, "Bloody hell, that man is Jesus Christ. I should send him a pint."

Not to be outdone, the Newfie looks over and says, "Well, b'y, I s'pose I should send him a shot of Screech."

After Jesus finishes his pint and his shot, he walks over to the Englishman and shakes his hand while thanking him for the pint.

The Englishman jumps up and shouts, "Thank you, Jesus, you cured my arthritis! I feel 20 years younger!"

Jesus turns and holds out his hand to the Newfie. The Newfie flips his chair over trying to back away, and says, "Screw dat, buddy. I'm on worker's compensation!"

June buys tickets to a Halloween party at the Lions Centre. Her husband doesn't want to go, and he has made it perfectly clear he thinks the party will be a waste of time. He makes fun of her for wanting to attend and won't help her pick a costume. Every idea June has for her husband, he shoots down. She asks if he wants to be Tarzan; he refuses. She asks if he wants to go as a vampire; he laughs in her face.

Eventually June gets fed up with trying to reason with her husband. She looks at him and says, "My son, I'm tellin' ya, we're going, and we're dressin' up, too. We is goin' as a horse. I'm gonna be the front, and you're gonna be yourself."

There is a big fire in a home out in Goulds, and the family loses everything they own. A reporter from NTV is sent to cover the story, and he manages to speak to the owner of the property.

Q: Why was the Newfie pushing his house down the hill?

A: He was trying to jump-start the furnace.

REPORTER: "I'm sorry you lost everything, sir. Will insurance cover what you and your family have lost?"

OWNER: "Insurance? Sure I never had dat. Waste o' money, to be sure."

REPORTER: "But what about your family? Surely they need reassurance that everything will be all right."

OWNER: "Nah, b'y, dey're all right."

REPORTER: "Sir, can you please tell our viewers how you and your family can put on such a brave face in the middle of this tragedy?"

OWNER: "Well, buddy, 'tis like this. I spent the last tree years cuttin' up lumber and storing it in the attic, and just last week I figured out dat der is 'nuff der to build a new house. Work starts on it 'ere tomorrow. Me wife and kids got no worries."

Garge pulls up a stool at his local bar.

The bartender looks at him and says, "My God, Garge, you looks some terrible t'day. Wha's the matter wit you?"

Garge shakes his head. "I'm gonna be a father, b'y."

The bartender puts out his hand. "Let me be the first to shake your hand. 'Tis awful good news."

Garge shakes his head again. "Not when the wife hears about it."

Q: Why did the Newfie cut a hole in his umbrella?

A: He wanted to know when it stopped raining.

A bayman pulls his truck up to the gate at the lumber yard. He gets out and shouts, "I needs some of dem der two-be-fars!"

The clerk looks at him and says, "Sir, do you mean two-by-fours?" The bayman points at his truck and replies, "Yes, b'y. Fill 'er up."

"Well, how long do you need them?" the clerk asks.

The bayman thinks for a moment and says, "By God, I'm buildin' a 'ouse outta dat wood, so I s'pose I needs 'em for a long time."

'Twas a real stormy night on the ferry crossing from Port aux Basques to North Sydney. The boat ride, which normally takes about four and a half hours to complete, was well into its sixth hour, and the ferry was no closer to shore than two hours previous. Suddenly, the ferry was hit broadside by a large wave, and it started to sink. The captain had to call an abandon ship. All the Newfies ran downstairs and piled into their cars.

A middle-aged Newfie woman goes to her doctor to see what can be done about reviving her husband's sex drive. She complains that her husband just isn't able to satisfy her anymore. The doctor suggests Viagra.

"Oh, no," says the woman. "Sure he won't even chew a baby aspirin, let alone swallow a pill like that."

"No worries," replies the doctor. "Just put it in his tea. That should fix things right up for you. Give me a call if you have any questions."

Not a week later, the woman calls the doctor, and he makes sure to ask about any progress in her love life.

Q: What did the Newfie say to his wife when he caught her in bed with another man?

A: "Look at buddy der, he t'inks he's me."

"Oh my gentle Jesus in garden, doctor," the woman says. "That was the most horrible thing that has ever happened to me."

"Oh my goodness," the doctor replies. "Tell me what happened."

"Well now, I did exactly as you says. I dropped that small pill into his tea, and away he went. He stood up straight as a poker and got a twinkle in his eye like I haven't seen in years. His zipper fair split apart at the sight of me. He picked me up and laid me across the table and sent all of the cups and spoons and everything flying in all directions. He ripped our clothes off right then an' there and made mad, passionate love to me on top of the table. It was terrifying," says the woman.

The doctor asks, "What was so terrible about the experience? Didn't you enjoy yourself?"

"Oh my, yes," says the woman. "That was the best sex I've ever had. But jumpin' holy Lord, sure they banned us from Tim Hortons for life, and me husband is still in jail."

Warning Signs You Might Be in Newfoundland

Found on the bottom of beer cans—Open Other End.

Directions found on a bar of soap—Use like regular soap.

Found on a hairdryer warning label—Do not use while sleeping.

Found on an iron label—Do not iron clothes on body.

Warning found on a bottle of sleeping pills—Might cause drowsiness.

Found on a can of beef stew—Product will be hot after heating.

Warning found on children's cough medicine—Do not operate a motor vehicle after ingesting.

A woman from Grand Falls goes to the local clinic where she is attended to by one of the youngest doctors on staff. She is only in the examination room for a minute or two when she runs from the room screaming and crying.

One of the older doctors the woman has seen on other occasions stops her to find out what's wrong. Through her tears she tells him what happened with the younger doctor.

The older doctor gets angry at what the woman says and walks back to the examination room to find the younger doctor. He doesn't bother knocking on the door, but just barges in the room and demands an explanation.

"What in the hell do you think you're doing telling a 65-year-old woman who has three children and six grandchildren that she is pregnant?" the older doctor asks.

The younger doctor looks up from his paperwork and smiles. "Ask her if her hiccups are gone."

A woman walks into a dress store on Water Street. She wants something special to wear when she goes out for dinner with her husband. The woman tries on several dresses, and when she finds the one that's the most flattering, she takes it to the clerk to pay for it. The clerk asks her how she wants to pay, and the woman takes out her credit card and passes it to the clerk.

The clerk notices the woman hasn't signed the back of the credit card, so she says, "Excuse me, dear, I can't accept this credit card. You haven't signed it on the back."

The woman asks, "Why? What's the difference?"

"Well," the clerk says, "I need to compare your signature on the card with what you write on the receipt."

So, the woman flips the credit card over and signs it in front of the clerk. The clerk verifies that the signatures match and the woman leaves the store with her new dress.

A woman marches into a drugstore in Gander and demands poison to kill her husband.

"What?" the pharmacist asks.

The woman announces to the whole store that her husband is cheating on her, and she wants to kill him.

The pharmacist tells her, "My dear woman, even if your husband is cheating on you, I can't sell you anything you would use to kill another person."

The woman reaches into her purse and pulls out a picture of her husband having sex with the pharmacist's wife.

The pharmacist quickly fills a bottle with pills and passes it to her. "Sorry," he says, "I didn't realize you had a prescription."

Wilf, an elderly Newfie, is on his deathbed. He hasn't said much over the past few days and seems to have accepted the inevitable. While he's contemplating death and the hereafter, he sniffs at a familiar smell wafting through the house. He can smell his favourite cookies baking in the kitchen. Wilf can't figure out if he's dreaming or not, so he manages to summon the last bit of strength left in his body to walk the short distance to the kitchen.

When he gets through the kitchen door, he's amazed to see what looks like a mountain of molasses jimmies sitting on the table. Wilf actually pinches himself to see if he's dreaming. He reaches out to pick up a cookie, but his hand is quickly slapped away by a spatula.

He looks up to see his wife of more than 50 years, standing beside the stove, with her hands on her hips. She says, "Wilf, what is you doin' out of yer bed? You knows you is sick."

Wilf replies, "Me dear, I smelled your cookies, and I had to come out here and get one. I just wanted one last taste before I go to meet my maker."

His wife says, "Listen here now, buddy, you keeps your hands off them cookies. They is for the funeral."

Buddy is stumbling along George Street when he spies a hooker lurking in the shadows. He hears a voice whisper "$20." Now, Buddy is usually pretty good about staying on the good side of the law, but he hasn't tried sex with a prostitute before so he decides to give it a go. Buddy starts having sex with the hooker, right in the alleyway. A light flashes on them. Of course, it's a police officer.

A gruff voice asks, "What's going on here?"

Buddy says, "I'm making love to my wife, officer."

The officer says, "Oh, I'm sorry. I didn't realize she was your wife."

Buddy scoffs. "Neither did I until you shone that light on her face."

Standing in the middle of the Village mall, Garge and his missus are having a terrible argument. His missus shouts, "I was a fool when I married you 20 years ago!"

Garge yells back, "Well there, missus, you might well have been. I was in love with you at the time, and I didn't notice."

A passenger in a taxicab in St. John's leans forward and taps the driver on the shoulder. He wants to ask the driver what time the pubs close on George Street.

The driver yells out and curses, his foot accidentally hits the gas and he almost hits a police car but manages to slam on the brakes and stop only a few inches from a light pole.

Both men are shaken up. The driver turns around and says, "My God, don't ever, ever do anything like that again. You just about killed us!"

The passenger apologizes and says he didn't think tapping anyone on the shoulder would cause that kind of reaction, especially in a cab.

The driver says, "My son, 'tis completely my fault. This right here is me first day driving a taxi. For the past 20 years, I've been workin' for a funeral home driving the hearse."

A Newfie gets a flat tire out on the highway. He pulls over to the side of the road and stops. The Newfie gets out of the car and picks as many wildflowers as he can find. He places half the flowers at the front bumper of car and the other half at the back. He gets back in the car and sits inside, waiting for help.

A Good Samaritan stops and asks if the Newfie needs help. The two men start changing the flat. The Good Samaritan asks the Newfie, "Why do you have flowers at the front and back of your car?"

The Newfie responds, "Well, b'y, I saw the ad on the TV. When you breaks down, you got to put flares in the front and flares it back. I don't rightly understand it, either."

A Newfie who has never travelled anywhere goes on vacation to St. John's. As he's walking through a store, he spies a mirror. He picks it up, looks at his reflection and says, "Good God, how did dey gets a snap of me fadder?"

The Newfie buys the mirror and heads for home. He remembers that his wife fair hated his father, so he puts the mirror up in the barn.

Now that the mirror is up, every morning before he goes fishing the Newfie takes the time to go out and gaze at the picture of his father. His wife soon gets to wondering what he's up to in the barn and figures he must be cheating on her.

She goes out to the barn, takes one look in the mirror and says, "Lard Jeezus, der's the old bitch that he's runnin' around wit."

A Newfie replaces all of his windows with new energy-efficient ones that are backed up with all kinds of guarantees and promises. A year to the day after the windows are installed, he starts getting threatening phone calls from the window contractor. The contractor keeps yelling at the Newfie, telling him he needs to pay for his new windows, or they will be removed from the house.

The Newfie replies, "Now you listen here, mister. You sold me windows that promised they would pay for themselves within a year..."

A travelling circus makes its way to St. John's and amazes the people with an elephant that can accurately indicate a person's age by stomping out the numbers on the ground. A Newfie sits and watches as a child stands in front of the elephant, and the elephant stomps his foot six times. The child verifies she's six years old. The Newfie can't believe what he sees.

Next in line, a man stands in front of the elephant and it stomps three times, pauses for a minute and then stomps four more times. The man verifies he is 34 years old. The Newfie shouts out that the elephant is cheating.

Q: Why couldn't the Newfie write the number 11?

A: He couldn't figure out which one went first.

The elephant trainer gets angry with the Newfie and drags him over to stand in front of the elephant. The elephant eyes the Newfie carefully. He lifts his tail and lets go of a fart like no one has ever heard before. Then he raises his huge foot and stomps twice.

The Newfie looks astounded. "By the Jesus, he's right. I turned farty-two on my birthday."

A Newfie winter statistic—98 percent of Canadians say, "Oh, crap!" just before ending up in a ditch off a slippery road. The other two percent are Newfies who say, "Hold on to dis beer and watch dis!"

He Was so Newfie that...

He tripped over a cordless-phone wire.

He spent 20 minutes staring at the juice container because it said "concentrate."

He told the mainlander to meet him at the corner of Walk and Don't Walk.

He asked for a price check at the dollar store.

He sold his car for gas money.

Two Newfies named Rodney and Joe are out ice fishing, and Rodney complains about his wife the whole time.

Rodney says, "B'y, I'm thinking about divorcing the wife. Sure she hasn't said not one word to me in over a month. I got no idea what to do about it."

Joe stops and thinks about what Rodney has told him and replies, "Rod b'y, be careful what you does in the situation. A good woman like that is some hard to find."

A Newfie groom is getting ready to be married when his best man from the mainland asks if the bride is pretty.

The groom tells his friend the bride is really nice, treats him really well.

The best man asks again if the bride is pretty.

"Well," the groom says, "put it this way. If beauty is a sin, she don't have to worry about that one."

A Newfie scientist who works for the Department of Fisheries in St. John's is waiting for 12 water samples to arrive at the lab. He can't continue his work until the samples arrive, so he goes out, gets a cup of coffee and sits back down at his desk. While he's drinking his coffee a flea happens to land on the papers in front of him.

He looks carefully at the flea and notices it has three sets of legs. Being a scientist, he decides to find out what will happen if he removes a set of legs. He rips off one set, puts the flea back on the table and tells it to jump over the ruler on his desk. To his surprise, the flea jumps over the ruler. The scientist records his notes.

He then removes the second set of legs, puts the flea back on the desk and tells it to jump over the ruler. The flea does it again. The scientist makes a few more notes and goes back to staring at the flea.

Finally, he removes the last set of legs, puts the flea back on the desk and tells it to jump over the ruler. This time nothing happens. The poor flea can't jump over the ruler. The scientist records his conclusion to the experiment: "For some unknown reason, when all of the legs have been removed from the common flea, it can't hear anymore."

An elderly Newfie woman runs through the halls of her nursing home every day wearing only a nightie. Every so often, she lifts the hem of her nightdress and says, "Supersex!"

One day she walks up to an older man in a wheel-chair. She flips up her gown, calls out "Supersex!" and walks away.

The older man sits quietly for a minute, looks up at the nurse and says, "I'll take the soup, please."

Freddie at the Head of the Class

Freddie isn't the most well-behaved student in class. It only took two days after returning from summer vacation for the teacher to start calling home about his behaviour.

Freddie's mother puts off talking with the teacher because she knows the teacher is going to tell her about how Freddie has done this bad thing or how Freddie had done that bad thing.

Finally, Freddie's teacher manages to get his mother on the phone. The teacher explains that Freddie has been misbehaving, and it is only the beginning of the school year.

After the teacher is finished with her speech, Freddie's mother says, "Hold on der, missus. I had Freddie here for two whole months, and not once did I call you to let you know when he done something wrong."

•

Besides getting into a lot of trouble at school, Freddie consistently gets poor marks. After failing three tests in a row, Freddie and his parents have a chat.

When Freddie gets to school the next morning, he walks up to his teacher and taps her on the shoulder. He says, "Miss, I don't want to make you afraid or nuthin', but me fadder told me last night that if I don't start getting better scores on me tests, someone is gonna get a licking."

•

The last straw for Freddie's teacher is when he manages to get only two percent on an English test. The teacher asks Freddie what he thinks the problem is.

Freddie says, "Miss, I don't know what's wrong. I tries to learn. I tries real hard, but everyt'ing you says goes in both ears and out the other."

Freddie's teacher looks puzzled and says, "Freddie, in both ears and out the other? You only have two ears, Freddie."

Freddie replies, "See, miss? I'm no good at math either."

You Might Be a Newfie if...

You live closer to England than to BC.

Your Trans Canada Highway includes a four-hour ferry ride.

You got your driver's licence without ever seeing a stoplight.

When you were growing up, being a fashionista meant getting new clothes from the Sears catalogue.

You buy groceries in a Dominion instead of a Safeway or Save-On-Foods.

You buy a new car every three years because your old car always rusts out.

You count moose as speed bumps.

You have never heard about plugging in your car when the winter temperature drops below −25° C.

Your provincial budget includes money to replace town signs stolen by tourists.

You have to teach your children to say "morning" instead of "marnin'."

The self-proclaimed fifth city of your province is located in Alberta.

You can count on one hand all the stop signs in your community.

A fisherman and his new wife are busy setting up house together when her mother comes to visit. She has barely walked into the house when she starts demanding that she inspect her daughter's new home from top to bottom. The fisherman has genuinely tried get along with his new mother-in-law. He wants to have a friendly relationship with her—he doesn't want to be one of those men who hates his mother-in-law, but it seems like nothing is working between them. His mother-in-law nags him every chance she gets. She demands that he renovate the house and buy new furniture. She criticizes everything he does and manages to make life almost unbearable for the fisherman and the love of his life.

On the third day of her visit, the fisherman shows his mother-in-law the brand new barn. In the barn, he keeps a donkey that's used to plough the small farm where he grows vegetables. During the mother-in-law's inspection of the barn, the donkey suddenly gets spooked and kicks the mother-in-law in the head. She dies almost instantly. Of course, the couple is in shock, and they soon forget how demanding and criticizing she was.

During the wake, the fisherman dutifully stands beside the casket and greets his friends and neighbours as they come to pay their respects.

The minister notices that whenever a woman whispers something to the farmer, he nods his head and says something. Whenever a man walks by and whispers to the farmer, he shakes his head and mumbles a reply.

Curious as to what's going on, the minister asks the fisherman what everyone is saying to him. The fisherman replies, "All de women come up and says, 'What a terrible tragedy,' and like a good son-in-law, I nod my head and says, 'Yes, missus, it sure is.' But de men come up to me and ask, 'Can I borrow dat der donkey of yours?' and I shake my head no and say, 'Can't, b'y, she's all booked up for the next year.'"

It's that time of year again, and a census worker walks up to a house in a small town in Newfoundland and knocks on the door.

The woman of the house answers, and the census worker asks her how many children she has and what their ages are.

The woman replies, "Let me t'ink about dis now. We got the twins, Millie and Billy, they're 34. And then there's the twins, Tess and Beth, they're 27. And then there's the twins, Frannie and Jenny, they're 24."

"Hold on! Hold on!" exclaims the census worker. "Did you have twins EVERY time?"

The woman answers, "Lardy jumpin' no, there were hundreds of times we didn't get nuthin'."

Two Newfies, one old and one young, are pushing their carts around Kent Building Supplies when they collide and spill the contents of their carts everywhere.

The old Newfie says to the young Newfie, "My God, I'm sorry about dat. I'm looking for my wife, and I wasn't paying no attention to where I was going."

The young Newfie says, "That's okay. What a coincidence. I'm wandering around looking for my wife, too. I'm getting a little desperate to find her."

The old Newfie says, "Well den, perhaps we can help each other out. Tell me what your wife looks like."

The young Newfie says, "Well, she's 26 years old, tall, beautiful, blonde hair, blue eyes, long legs and big boobs, and today she's wearing tight shorts, a halter top and no bra. Tell me what your wife looks like."

The old Newfie answers, "Doesn't matter now. Let's find yours."

A Newfie walks into the welfare office and asks for help. The clerk tells him to fill out a questionnaire before his interview. One of the questions asks him to explain why he needs help. The Newfie thinks for a moment before writing down his answer: "I've been having lots of trouble with me eyes. I just can't see meself going to work."

A Newfie working in Calgary is sitting in a local bar when he gets a call on his cell phone. The Newfie gets really excited and orders beer for everyone in the bar. Once the beers are poured and passed around, he announces that his wife gave birth to a typical baby boy that weighs 25 pounds.

The bar patrons cannot believe that 25 pounds is typical, so they ask the Newfie about it.

The Newfie says, "Listen here, b'ys, that's just about right. We grows 'em healthy down east."

A few weeks later, the Newfie wanders back into the bar. The bartender recognizes him immediately and asks where he has been. The Newfie tells the bartender he just got back from a trip to see his wife and new baby.

The bartender says, "Goodness me, if your son was 25 pounds when he was born, how heavy is he two weeks later?"

The Newfie responds, "B'y, they weighed him just this morning and he is 17 pounds."

The bartender looks confused and asks, "What happened? Has the little fellow been sick?"

The Newfie proudly replies, "Nah, b'y. We just had him circumcised, that's all."

Two baymen brothers are bored so they decide to make their own fun. They come up with the wonderful idea of knocking over the outhouse. The boys make sure no one is watching, sneak up behind the outhouse and give it a mighty shove. Over it goes, and the boys quickly run into the woods. After about an hour of sitting around and laughing, they saunter home as if nothing happened.

As soon as they walk in the door, their father calls them into the front room. He stands up—holding his belt—as they walk through the door.

Q: How do you drive a Newfie crazy?

A: Put him in a round room and tell him to sit in the corner.

He yells, "Did you b'ys tip over the outhouse this afternoon?"

The older brother says, "Fadder b'y, I can't tell a lie. Yes, sir, we was the ones who pushed over the outhouse earlier today."

The boys' father, angry about the fact that they tipped over the outhouse, gives them a licking and sends them to bed without any supper.

The next morning, the boys creep into the kitchen, hoping to avoid their father, but there he is, large as life, seated at the kitchen table.

He looks up from his breakfast and says, "'Ave you b'ys learned your lesson?"

"We have, fadder," says one of the sons, "but in church we learned that if you do something wrong and truthfully admit it, the priest forgives you, and so you shouldn't be punished. How come we got a licking and sent to bed with no supper?"

"Ha!" says the father. "That priest wasn't in the outhouse when you pushed it over."

Randy applies for a job, but the foreman flat-out refuses to employ him unless he passes a math test. Randy starts grumbling under his breath about mainlanders stealing jobs on The Rock, but realizes he has to go through with the test because he really needs the work.

The foreman passes Randy a piece of paper and says, "Okay, your first question: Without using numbers, represent the number nine."

"Without numbers?" Randy asks. "Dat's pretty easy." He draws three trees on the page.

"What in the hell is this?" the boss asks.

"My God, b'y, can't you count? Tree and tree and tree makes nine," says the Newfie.

"Well, okay, fair enough," says the boss. "Now for your second question. Using the same rules, draw 99 for me."

Randy stares off into space for a while, and then makes a smudge across each tree. "Der you go, laddie," Randy says proudly.

The boss scratches his head, then squints at the picture and asks, "How on earth do you think that represents the number 99?"

Randy answers, "Each of dem der trees is dirty now. So, it's dirty-tree and dirty–tree and dirty-tree. Dat der equals 99, buddy."

The boss starts getting worried that he might have to give the Newfie the job, so he says, "All right, last math question, same rules again, but represent the number 100."

The Newfie thinks for a few minutes and then makes a little mark at the bottom of each tree and says, "Der you go, b'y. One hundred."

The boss looks at the picture again and says, laughing, "You must be crazier than I am if you think that represents 100!"

Randy, not to be outdone by a mainlander, leans forward and points to the marks at the bottom of each tree and says, "A tiny dog came along and took a shit by each tree. So listen close to what you got now, buddy. You've got a dirty-tree-and-a-turd, dirty-tree-and-a-turd and dirty-tree-and-a-turd. Dat makes 100 all together. So where do I pick up me first cheque?"

A Newfie is about to suffer a terrible accident while walking down the street: he tosses his smoke into an open manhole and then tries to step on the butt.

A husband and wife are on their way to visit friends around the bay. As they are driving down the dirt road leading to their friends' house, they get bogged down in a muddy spot on the road. After a few minutes of spinning the car's tires, the couple gives up trying to get themselves out of the rut. Eventually, they see a man coming toward them on his quad.

He stops when he sees the couple in trouble and is kind enough to help them pull the car out.

When the car is free and the couple is ready to be on their way, the husband passes the man $50 for helping them.

The man turns to the husband and says, "You know, buddy, you guys is the umpteenth car I've helped out of the mud today."

The husband looks around him and says, "My goodness, after helping people out of the mud, when do you have time to do all your other work? You must work straight through the night."

The man replies seriously, "No, b'y. I does all me work in the day. Night is when I puts the water in that hole."

The owner of a golf course in St. John's gets confused over an invoice he's supposed to pay by the end of the week. He finally accepts that he needs help figuring out what to do, so he calls his assistant into his office.

He says to her, "I need some help with a math question. You graduated from MUN, so I figure you're the best one to ask. If I give you $30,000, minus 16 percent, how much do you take off?"

The assistant only has to think about her answer for a second. She answers, "I'd take off everything but me earrings."

Newfie Computer Terms

LOG ON: Dat'll make the wood stove hotter.

MONITOR: Keep dem eyes on dat wood stove.

LOG OFF: De wood stove is good and hot now, b'y.

SCREEN: What you shuts to keep the nippers out.

SCREEN SAVER: What you uses to fix the screen when the nippers break through.

BYTE: What the damn nippers does.

BIT: What the damn nippers done last night.

CHIP: What we eats watchin' hockey.

MICROCHIP: What's left in the chip bag when the game's over.

MOUSE: What eats trew da cereal box.

CURSOR: Buddy over der that cusses all the time.

ONLINE: Damn good sign that we'll have clean clothes this week.

OFFLINE: When the pins lets go, and the clothes falls in the dirt.

A priest walking down a back lane spies a young man trying to load hay onto a cart. The priest surmises that the hay must have fallen off the cart, and the young man needs to pick it up before going any further.

The priest calls out to the young Newfie. "My son, that looks like mighty hard work. Sit down and rest a spell, and I'll help you pick up the rest of your hay."

The young Newfie shakes his head and says, "Thanks anyway, but fadder wouldn't like me taking your help."

"Don't be silly," the priest says. "Every one of God's creatures can take a break from hard labour. Come sit with me and have a drink of water."

Again the young Newfie tells the priest that his father will get angry with him if he sits down and takes a break.

The priest gets upset at the thought of the Newfie not even stopping for a sip of water. He looks at him and says, "I can't imagine why you have such a low opinion of your father. Surely he is a good man who would offer you a drink himself if he were here. Let me know where I can find him so we can discuss his treatment of you like men."

"Well, look here, priest," replies the young Newfie. "You wants to find fadder? Sure 'nuff he's under the hay."

A man and his wife move back home to Newfoundland. The man is reluctant to change their insurance policy because his wife has a wooden leg, and in Ontario it was $2000 a year to insure. The man is positive that it's going be much more in Newfoundland.

Eventually, the insurance agency in Ontario informs the couple that they must seek coverage from an agency that's located in their province of residence.

The man and his wife go get a quote from a local agency. The agent looks up the cost of insuring the wooden leg and finds out that it's only $39 per year.

The man is shocked at the price difference. He says to the agent, "Wow, that sure is a huge difference from Ontario! Why is the insurance so cheap in Newfoundland?"

The agent shrugs her shoulders and says, "Sir, I don't know what the difference is, but right here on my screen it says, 'Any wooden structure, with a sprinkler system over it, is $39.'"

George is a patient on the ward for the mentally ill at the Waterford Hospital in St. John's.

One day while he's walking past the hospital swimming pool, another patient jumps into the deep end. He sinks to the bottom and stays there. He doesn't even try to swim, so George jumps in the pool to save him. He swims to the bottom and pulls the other patient out.

When his doctor becomes aware of George's heroic act, he immediately signs the order to have George discharged from the hospital. The doctor notes that because George had the presence of mind to save someone else, he is deemed mentally stable.

When the doctor goes to tell George the news, he says, "George, I have good news for you and bad news for you. The good news is you're being discharged today because you were able to respond rationally to a crisis. By jumping in and saving another patient, I have come to the conclusion that you now display sound thinking and judgment. The bad news is the patient that you dragged out of the pool hung himself in the bathroom right after you saved him. I am really sorry, but he passed away."

George looks surprised at the doctor's news and says, "Doc, that feller didn't hang hisself; I put him up there to dry. So, when can I go home?"

Two Newfies go for a dip at the local swimming hole. When they reach the best place to jump off the rocks, they find a woman crying and looking desperately into the water. The woman tells them her boyfriend has just disappeared under the water, and she can't see him anymore. One of the Newfies quickly jumps in to try and find the boyfriend. After about a minute, he pulls out a man who is obviously not breathing. The Newfie starts giving the man mouth-to-mouth but nothing seems to help. The woman has become hysterical during the whole rescue, and she starts crying harder than ever.

After a few minutes, she asks, "Is he gonna be okay?"

The Newfie calls over his shoulder, "It doesn't look too good, missus. He hasn't responded to nuttin' I've done, and his breath is really bad."

The woman looks through her tears and says, "Ummm, that's not my boyfriend. It's a man who was lost through the ice about a year ago..."

One night while driving into town, two Newfies witness a moose accident on the TCH. As they are hurtling over the Trans Canada doing a respectable 10 kilometres an hour over the speed limit, they see a sedan pull out to pass a Newfoundland Hydro truck. The truck swerves to miss a moose, and the sedan swerves to miss the Hydro truck. Unfortunately, missing the Hydro truck means hitting the moose. It is the most spectacular moose accident the two Newfies have ever witnessed. The sedan hits the moose in the hindquarters, its head swings back and shatters the windshield and the moose then flies over the top of the car and lands on the truck.

At the sight of the accident, the Newfies stop their car and sit there, stunned. The passenger grabs the driver's arm and says, "Come on, you knows first aid. You got to go over there!"

The driver slowly shakes his head and says, "I ain't doing first aid on no moose!"

Top 10 Reasons
Why Being a Newfie "Rocks"

1. We live on an island—it's harder for everyone else to get here.

2. We have our own dictionary—no one can understand us, but we understand ourselves just fine.

3. We are brave enough to stand up to PETA and Paul McCartney—take *that* chicken, beef and pork producers.

4. We have our own rum, and we admit it tastes pretty horrible, but we still convince tourists they have to drink it in order to become honorary Newfies.

5. We have the most pubs per square-foot in Canada.

6. We get made fun of all the time; that lets us make fun of anyone we want.

7. We observe traditions that most of Canada has never heard of.

8. We may not have come over on the *Mayflower*, but we can trace our ancestry to some of the first settlers in North America.

9. We are one of the smallest provinces by population, but most Canadians know at least one Newfie.

10. We will beat you at drinking, church bingos and telling Newfie jokes.

Bob is a Newfie who has never really been away from home. He has never travelled, and he has never stayed in a hotel. If fact, Bob has never even spent the night in a hospital. To put it mildly, Bob is unaware of the workings of life outside his own home. One night when he is well over 50 years old, Bob and his wife go to visit their grandchildren and have to stay overnight in a motel because of a snowstorm. When Bob gets home, someone asks him how he enjoyed his night in the motel.

Bob replies, "B'y, we walked into that room and there it was, two beds all made up and everything!"

A stray cat is found hanging around a house in Newfoundland. The mother of the house, not wanting another stray cat in the community, calls the SPCA to find out what she can do with the cat.

The person from the SPCA instructs her to take the cat in for adoption, and tells her to load it into a milk container for transport.

The mother gets off the phone, confused. "A milk carton, that's what she says. I can't believe the SPCA goes on about cruelty to animals and they're telling us to squash a little cat into a milk carton!"

Eventually, the mother calls the SPCA back to clarify what they mean. The clerk laughs and says, "No, I mean the container that the milk cartons come in. You know, the big plastic one with all the holes in it."

A Newfie looks at his friend and says, "Jack, my b'y, how come you looks right sad today?"

Jack looks at the Newfie and replies, "Well, I just come back from me doctor, and he gave me a list of t'ings that's wrong. I got heart problems, arthritis, high blood pressure and a brain tumour that they can't do nuttin' for. I could die any day a'toll."

The Newfie says, "Jack b'y, dat's horrible news, but I guess it could be worse."

Jack says, "Worse b'y, it already got worse. The bank took me 'ouse, and the wife up and left with the kids. I got nuttin' left to live fer."

The Newfie says, "Jack b'y, dat's more terrible news, but I guess it still could be worse."

Jack fair yells, "B'y, what do you mean it could be worse? What's worse than all the t'ings that's goin' wrong wit me?"

The Newfie smiles and says, "Well den, Jack me buddy, it could be me!"

A minister boards an airplane for St. John's. He has the good fortune to be seated next to a Newfie. The minister and the Newfie are having a fine chat until the flight attendant comes around and asks them if they want anything to drink. The Newfie decides because he's still on vacation, a rum and Coke is what he wants. The flight attendant gives him the drink and asks the minister what he would like. The minister asks for a glass of water.

When the attendant turns away to get the water, the minister looks at the Newfie and says, "I would rather fornicate with 10 whores and know that my soul was damned before I would let a drop of liquor pass through my lips." He finishes his sentence just as the attendant hands him his water.

The Newfie quickly passes his rum and Coke back to the attendant and says, "Sure, buddy, I would too. I just didn't know that was a choice we had."

A Newfie has gained a fair amount of weight, so his doctor makes him go on a diet.

The doctor explains, "I want you to eat regularly for two days, then skip a day. If you repeat this for two weeks, you should lose at least five pounds by the next time I see you."

Two weeks after the Newfie starts the diet, he walks into the doctor's office. The doctor is shocked that the Newfie had lost almost 50 pounds. "This is one of the most amazing things I have ever seen! Did you follow my instructions exactly?" asks the doctor.

The Newfie looks at his doctor while nodding his head and says, "Yessir, I sure did follow what you says. I figured I was gonna drop dead by the end of the terd day."

The doctor asks, "Do you mean drop dead from the hunger?"

"No," the Newfie replies, "from all that skippin' you made me do."

Jim dies in a horrible car crash, and his wife is in such a state that the Health Sciences Centre morgue sends for Jim's two best friends to come and identify the body. The attendant walks the first friend to the body and pulls back the sheet.

Jim's buddy says, "Well then, sir, the only way I gots to figure out if dat's Jim is to roll him over."

The attendant rolls over the body.

"Nope," the first friend says, "this here's not Jim."

The attendant looks at the first friend strangely and decides he should see what the other friend has to say.

The attendant walks the second friend to the body and pulls back the sheet.

Jim's other buddy says, "Look here, sir, the only way I can see if dat's Jim is to roll him over."

Q: A Newfie and a mainlander are both thrown from a building. Who hits the ground first?

A: The mainlander—the Newfie has to go back and ask for directions.

The attendant rolls over the body.

"Nope," the second friend says, "I knows dat ain't Jim."

The attendant is confused. He asks them how they can tell the body isn't Jim's.

One of the friends says, "Well, sir, Jim has two assholes."

"What? He has two assholes?" exclaims the attendant.

"Yup, everyone 'round here knows he has two assholes, too. It weren't no secret. Every single time we all went down to George Street, people says, 'Here comes Jim with them two assholes.'"

One night Millie calls Dave in quite a state. He isn't home so she has to leave a message: "Dave, me son, I needs you to get your arse over 'ere for visit, and for the love of God, 'dis time don't forget the protection."

Dave gets the message when he arrives home from work. He takes a shower and makes his way over to Millie's.

Millie opens the door and there is Dave, standing in front of her with his 12-gauge shotgun under his arm.

The front-desk clerk at the Delta Hotel in St. John's is being friendly to Stephen Harper while he's on a visit to Newfoundland. The two of them start swapping jokes back and forth until they're laughing so hard they can't stand up.

The clerk says, "I have a riddle. My mother and father had a baby. It wasn't my brother, and it wasn't my sister. Who was it?"

"I don't know," says Mr. Harper.

The clerk replies, "It was me." They both have a great laugh at the joke.

When Mr. Harper returns to Ottawa, he's sitting with a reporter before an interview about the newest budget. To lighten the mood, he decides to try out a joke on the reporter.

Mr. Harper says to the journalist, "My mother and father had a baby. It wasn't my brother and it wasn't my sister. Who was it?"

The reporter looks at him strangely and answers, "I don't know. Who was it?"

Mr. Harper looks at the reporter and replies, "A clerk from the Delta Hotel."

Todd, a Newfie who is known for getting drunk on George Street, stands up to leave the bar and falls flat on his face. After spending a few minutes trying to get up, he decides to crawl home.

The next morning, his wife shakes him awake and says, "You got drunk at the pub again and crawled home, didn't you?"

He looks up at his wife and says, "Yes, but how did you figure it out?"

She shakes her head and replies, "B'y, you left your wheelchair at the bar again."

Marge and her granddaughter Effie are sitting on the beach, staring at the moon. "Granny," Effie says, "wa's closer, T'ronto or the moon?"

Marge looks down at Effie and replies, "Maid, the moon got to be closer, sure; we can't see T'ronto from 'ere."

The Bank of Montreal is running a password audit and finds that Stevie O'Toole from Conception Bay, Newfoundland, is using the following password: MickeyDonaldMinnieGoofyDaffyBugsElmer-PlutoOttawa.

When Stevie is asked why he has such a long password, he replies, "Lord t'underin' Jeesus! Are yez blind or stupid? I was told me password had to be at least eight characters long wit' one capital."

CHAPTER EIGHT

Newfies on the Mainland

So sure, Newfies at home are pretty "comfortable." But, when they leave the island, look out because then they become just plain funny. If you ever get the chance, watch a bayman on his first trip off the island. Believe me, you'll understand…

A gas station just outside Halifax is desperately trying to increase its sales. They've tried a lot of different advertising gimmicks, but so far nothing has worked. The owner finally gets the grand idea of putting up a sign that reads, "Free sex with fill-up." Almost immediately the gas station's sales increase.

A Newfie pulls into the station, fills his truck with gas and asks the attendant for his free sex. The attendant tells him to pick a number between 1 and 10, and if he's right, he'll get free sex.

"I says…today, it's six, b'y," the Newfie guesses.

The attendant shakes his head and says, "Not today. You were close, though. The number was five. Maybe next time."

The next week, the same Newfie comes along with his buddy, fills up the tank and asks for the free sex.

The attendant tells him to pick a number between 1 and 10, and if he is right, he'll get free sex.

The Newfie guesses. "I says…today, it's two, b'y."

The attendant shakes his head and says, "Not today. You were close, though. The number was three. Maybe next time."

Q: What do you call someone stranded at the ferry terminal in Nova Scotia?

A: A Newfie who spent his ferry money on beer.

The Newfie looks at his buddy and says, "I thinks this here game might be rigged. I don't think that they gives away any sex for free."

His buddy looks at him and replies, "No, b'y, I'm sure that it ain't rigged. Me wife managed to win twice last week."

After committing horrible crimes in Los Angeles, a Torontonian, an American and a Newfoundlander are all sentenced to death. On the day of their executions, the men are informed they each get to decide how they want to die. They can choose death by lethal injection, the electric chair or hanging.

The American is too afraid of needles for lethal injection, and he doesn't like the idea of a hanging, so he chooses the electric chair.

He takes a deep breath, accepts his fate and sits down in the chair. The executioner pulls the switch, but nothing happens. The American just sits there. The executioner tries a second time, and still nothing happens. He tells the American that if it doesn't work on the third try, he will be a free man. The executioner pulls the switch, and nothing happens, so the American walks away from the prison.

The Torontonian also claims he's too afraid of needles for lethal injection and that he doesn't like the idea of a hanging, either, so he decides to die by the electric chair. Once again, the executioner tries three times to electrocute the criminal, but the chair doesn't work, so the Torontonian is set free.

The third person up for execution is the Newfie. He is asked how he wants to die. The Newfie thinks about it for a minute and responds, "Well, b'y, I don't like the needles, and since the electric chair don't work, I s'pose you're gonna have to hang me."

A Newfie walks into a bar in Saint John, New Brunswick, and orders three pints of beer. The bartender pours the beers and hands them to the Newfie. The Newfie picks up his pints and makes his way to the back of the bar. He sits down by himself and drinks the three pints by taking a sip from each beer until they are all finished. The Newfie walks back to the bar and orders three more. The bartender watches him return to his table and repeat the process of drinking the pints by taking sips from each glass until they are all finished.

Finally the bartender goes up and talks to the Newfie. He says, "Sir, draft beer goes flat pretty fast. I think it would taste better if you just bought one beer at time."

The Newfie replies, "Well, sir, 'tis like this. I got two brothers. One is in Toronto, the other is in Edmonton, and I'm here in Saint John. We made a promise to each other that we would drink beers like this so we could remember the good times we had when we lived at home. So you sees, I drinks a beer for each of us to remember the good old days back on The Rock."

The bartender tells the Newfie that it seems like a fine idea to remember his brothers in this way and that he'll never bring it up again.

The Newfie becomes a regular at the bar, and the bartender gets used to him ordering his three drinks and sipping at them one by one until they are finished. One day, though, the Newfie comes in, sits at the bar and only orders two pints. Everyone else who is used to the Newfie notices something is wrong.

When the Newfie orders another round of two pints, the bartender looks at him and says, "I'm sorry for your loss, but I just wanted to offer my condolences for your brother."

The Newfie looks confused for a minute, and then he laughs at the bartender. "Oh no, b'y, all me brothers is just fine. It's just that me wife has been saved, and she forced me to quit drinking. It hasn't affected me brothers, though."

A German, a Frenchman and a Newfie all meet up while camping in Jasper National Park. The German has brought vodka to drink, the Frenchman has brought champagne and the Newfie has brought a bottle of Screech. After a few rounds, they are getting drunk.

Suddenly, the German takes a shot from his bottle, throws it up in the air and shoots it. Glass and vodka explode all over the campsite.

The Newfie looks at him and says, "My God, b'y! What did you do dat fer?"

The German replies, "Vodka is so plentiful in my country, we can waste it and not care."

Next the Frenchman takes a swig from his bottle, throws it up in the air and shoots it. Once again the campers are covered with bits of glass and the remaining champagne.

The shocked Newfie calls out, "Lordy jumpin' dyin'! What did you do dat fer?"

The Frenchman replies, "Champagne is more plentiful than water in my country. We can throw it away, and there will always be more."

The Newfie eyes his two companions. He nurses his bottle of Screech for hours, and when he takes the last drop, he lays down the bottle and shoots the Frenchman.

The surprised German yells, "Why did you shoot him?"

The Newfie quickly answers, "Buddy, 'tis like dis. Where I comes from dat bottle is worth a nickel, and dat Frenchman ain't worth a damn."

Willy and his friend are visiting a fancy museum on the mainland when they both become fascinated with an exhibit from Ancient Egypt. They can't take their eyes off a mummy case that's dated 1263 BC.

Willy says to his friend, "What do you figure those numbers there mean?"

His buddy looks at him and replies, "Well now, Willy, I'm not too sure, but I wonder if they is the licence plate number of the truck that hit that poor feller over there."

A Newfie walks into a shop in Vancouver. The clerk notices his accent and asks him where he is from. The Newfie proudly tells her he is from Victoria, BC.

She tells him she is also from Victoria, but she has never heard anyone in BC talk like him.

The Newfie looks surprised, and says, "My God, maid. I never told you I was from here. I told you I was from Victoria, BC. I means Behind Carbonear."

A woman from the mainland marries a Newfie, and they move into a small apartment in Edmonton. She isn't the best housekeeper, and is oblivious to the accumulation of dust.

One day she gets a burst of energy and cleans the whole apartment from top to bottom. Later that evening when her husband gets home, he calls from the hallway, "Missus, what did you do with all the dust on the table here?"

She responds brightly, "I cleaned it."

He answers, "Damn, I had a phone number written there."

A mainlander overhears a Newfie yelling at a waitress in a restaurant on Yonge Street in Toronto. The Newfie is so mad that he has almost made the waitress cry.

The mainlander leans over to the Newfie and whispers, "Sir, you get more flies with honey than you do with vinegar."

The Newfie looks at the mainlander and says, "Of course dat's true. But what in the hell can I do with a bunch of flies?"

The police are called in when three bodies turn up at the morgue in Fort McMurray. The dead bodies are all men, and each one has a huge grin on his face. The police need to know what happened to the deceased, so the coroner reports his findings:

"First man, Frenchman, approximately 65 years old, died of cardiac arrest while making love to his wife.

"Second man, Scotsman, approximately 25 years old, according to the receipts in his pocket he won some money in the lottery, spent it all on whiskey. He died of alcohol poisoning.

"Third man, Newfie, 35 years old. He was struck by lightning and died."

The policeman says, "Wait a minute, doc. You say they all died with huge grins on their faces. I understand the Frenchman and Scot, but what did the Newfie have to be happy about?"

"Ah," the coroner replies. "He thought someone was taking his picture."

A Newfie is walking past a U-pick fruit orchard in British Columbia. He goes up to the attendant and asks how much the apples cost.

The attendant quotes the going rate. "The apples are all you can pick for $5."

The Newfie pulls some money out of his pocket and hands it to the attendant. "Okay," says the Newfie, "give me $10 worth."

A Newfie is away from home for the first time. One of the mainlanders he meets asks him politely where he's from, knowing full well his new acquaintance is from The Rock.

"Dildo," the Newfie answers.

The mainlander asks, "Why don't they change the name of that town?"

The Newfie responds, "Why would they bother to change the name?"

"Well," the mainlander says, "you know what it means."

The Newfie laughs. "What would they change it to? Vibrator Cove?"

A Newfie and his wife are looking at buying a piece of property just outside Edson in Alberta. After looking on the Internet for several months, they think they have found the perfect location. The Internet pictures show a lovely little house with a few acres that look perfect for planting the vegetable garden they have been wanting for years. Excited to see the place, they call a local real estate agent and make an appointment to see the piece of land.

When they arrive at the lot, the reality is completely different from the pictures they saw on the computer. In those photos, the land was green and covered with grass; there was a small creek running through the property and everything looked lush. In truth, the little piece of heaven is a disaster. The ground is dried up and brown, the creek is nothing more than a ditch and it appears as though even the weeds have trouble lasting in the soil.

The overexcited real estate agent has his heart set on making this sale. He looks at the couple and says, "Now folks, all this land really needs is a little water, a nice cool breeze and some good people."

The man eyes the salesman and replies, "Yes, b'y, I can see where you're comin' from, and I totally agrees wit ya. But then again, can't you say the same t'ing 'bout hell?"

Three guys are walking along the Rideau Canal. One is a Newfie, one is a Quebecer and the other is a Torontonian. They come across a lamp, and for the fun of it, the Torontonian rubs it. A genie pops out and promises to give each man one wish.

The Torontonian says, "I was born in Toronto when the air was still clean enough to take a deep breath. I wish there was no more smog." Poof! The air in Toronto is clean.

The Quebecer turns to the genie and says, "I want nothing more than for Quebec to be separate from Canada. Please build a wall around Quebec." Poof! A wall instantly appears, separating Quebec from the rest of Canada.

The Newfie rolls his eyes at the Quebecer, looks at the genie and asks, "So, what's up with that there wall, buddy?"

The genie replies, "Well, the wall is about 100 feet high and 50 feet thick, so nothing can get in or out of Quebec."

"All right then, me son," the Newfie says. "Fill 'er up."

A Newfie goes into a used-car dealership in Scarborough, Ontario. He is looking to buy a car he can drive to Newfoundland. The salesman shows him a car that's $2000. He tells the Newfie it's a pretty good car that has air conditioning, to boot. The Newfie asks him for something cheaper, so the salesman shows him a car that he says runs okay and doesn't have air conditioning but is only $1000. The Newfie asks for something cheaper. The salesman leads him to the back of the lot and shows him a car that runs but doesn't go in reverse. It's only $500.

The Newfie says, "Sold. I ain't comin' back here anyways."

A Newfie gets hired on a potato farm in PEI. He accepts the job of sorting all the potatoes the farmer harvests. The farmer gives the Newfie strict instructions to make three piles: one for small potatoes, one for medium-sized potatoes and one for large potatoes.

After sorting potatoes for a few hours, the Newfie walks up to the farmer, takes off his gloves and quits outright. The farmer looks at the Newfie and notices he's sweating and appears confused.

The farmer asks the Newfie, "Son, is the work too hard for you?"

The Newfie replies, "No, b'y, but all dem decisions is killing me."

A Newfie goes on vacation to Oklahoma City. He's sitting in a bar soaking up the local culture when a man comes in and sits next to him. The man goes on and on and on about how much land he owns. He boasts that he owns a huge ranch, and that his land goes as far as the eye can see.

Eventually, he asks the Newfie if he owns any land in Canada. The Newfie tells him he owns exactly 500 square feet of good old Newfie rock.

The man finds this hilarious. He slaps the Newfie on the back and says, "Five hundred square feet, that's my front porch! You can get in a truck and drive for five days and still not reach the end of my ranch."

The Newfie looks at him and responds, "Yes, b'y. I used to have a truck like dat, too."

A Newfie and two mainlanders are sitting in a bar in North Bay, Ontario. A local man walks in, and they all notice he doesn't have any ears. The bartender walks up to the three men and bets that if either of them can ask the local a question about his ears and not get beaten up, that man's drinks are on the house.

The first mainlander walks up to the local and says, "Don't you love the sound of thunder during a rainstorm?"

The local man takes the mainlander outside and beats him up pretty good.

The second mainlander walks up to the local and says, "What's your favourite song to listen to when you're dancing?"

The local man takes the other mainlander outside and beats him to within an inch of his life.

Q: Why did the Newfies get excited when they heard Quebec was separating from Canada?

A: Because it was only going to take an hour and a half to get to Toronto.

The Newfie is determined to get his drinks for free, so he watches the local man for a few minutes. He notices the man squints as he reads the label on his beer. The Newfie walks up to him and says, "Do you wear contact lenses?"

"Yes," the local man says. "How did you know?"

The Newfie looks at him and says, "Well, if you had ears, you'd be wearing your glasses."

Robbie and Melv set their minds to it and decide to leave Newfoundland and move to Alberta. They both figure they can get jobs out on the oil sands.

Before they leave to get on the plane, Robbie's dad gives the two young men some sage advice: "You b'ys watch out for dose mainlander cab drivers. If you gives dem an inch, dey'll take a mile. Every single one of dem will rob the two of you blind. Der's not much you can do about it. See, you calls for one, and dey tries to charge you whatever dey wants. Dat's pretty much the law of the jungle on the mainland. Jus' remember, don't you two fools pay dem exactly what dey asks. You makes sure dat you gets dem to a lower price."

After arriving at the airport in Fort McMurray, Robbie and Melv walk up to a cab and tell the driver they need to go to their hotel.

When they reach the front door of the hotel, the cabbie says, "That'll be $30, boys."

"Dat you don't den, buddy! My dad warned me about the likes of you. You'll only be getting $25 from me," says Robbie.

"And I'm only giving you $25, too," says Melv.

Two Newfies are stationed in a war zone. They figure they are doing their duty for Canada but often find they are pretty bored. One day, the Newfies spy a large group of the enemy marching down the road, so they hide behind a hill. Once the enemy is close enough, one of the Newfies yells, "One Newfie is better than 10 of you fellers!"

The enemy commander chooses 10 of his toughest soldiers and sends them in to fight the Newfies. The enemy runs over the hill, there's some gunfire and loud screaming and then nothing but silence.

The second Newfie gets brave and yells, "One Newfie is better than 100 of you fellers!"

The enemy commander has no choice but to send 100 of his soldiers over the hill. The soldiers go into battle without question. This time, the fight seems to last a few more minutes. The commander soon sees one of his soldiers crawling back to him.

The soldier gasps, "Don't send any more of our men. There's two of them over there."

A family moves from Fortune, Newfoundland, to Edmonton, Alberta. Their little son starts going to school, and it doesn't take long before the other kids begin to pick on him for being from Newfoundland.

One of the mainland kids' favourite jokes is to hold up a nickel and a dime and ask the Newfie boy, "Hey, do you want the biiiiiig nickel or the smaaaaaall dime?" Much to the delight of the other boys, the Newfie always picks the nickel instead of the dime.

The teacher finally gets fed up with watching the scene play out every day, so she takes the Newfie boy aside to talk to him.

Q: What do you call it when a Newfie loses his accent?

A: Artificial intelligence.

She says, "You're a big boy now, almost 10 years old. You must know the difference between a nickel and a dime. Why do you let the other boys tease you every single day?"

The Newfie boy responds, "Yes, miss, of course I knows the difference between a nickel and a dime. But, you knows dis is true too, if I ever takes that dime, them boys will stop passing me nickels."

During a Newfie's first trip to Toronto, he's parked on Queen Street and sees a broken-down truck that has several penguins in the back. Even the Newfie thinks it's a bit odd to see penguins in the back of a truck in Toronto, so he asks the driver what's going on. The driver informs the Newfie that the penguins are on their way to the zoo. The Newfie has never been to a zoo, so he asks if the driver wants any help with the delivery. The driver accepts and hands the penguins over to the Newfie. He gives the Newfie exact directions to the zoo and passes him $100 for helping him out. The men part ways and the driver assumes

the Newfie will get the penguins to the zoo without too much trouble.

Not long after, the driver sees the Newfie walking
along the sidewalk, with the penguins following him.

The driver pulls up beside the Newfie and calls
out, "Hey, didn't you take those penguins to the
zoo like we agreed?"

The Newfie quickly replies, "Yes, sir, I did. But
you see, I had some money left over after filling me
tank with gas so we're all going to the movies."

A Newfie is hired at a construction job site in
Calgary. His first task is to carry two-by-fours to
the first floor of the building. After 20 minutes of
observation, the foreman calls the Newfie over and
asks him why he is only carrying one two-by-four,
and the other workers are carrying two. The Newfie looks at the foreman and says, "Me son, I don't
rightly know what's wrong with them. I s'pose
they're just too lazy to make more than one trip."

A Newfie ends up at the emergency room in
Calgary. After several tests, the doctors have
to admit they aren't sure what's wrong with him,
so the Newfie is told he has to stay in the hospital. His
time there is horrible. The food is bland, the nurses
are mean and the TV doesn't work. By the end of

the week, the Newfie is in a fair state indeed. He keeps asking when he can go home.

The doctor finally comes to see him and tells the Newfie he has bad news.

The Newfie says, "Okay, doc, let me have it."

"You only have 36 hours to live. I'm sorry," the doctor says.

The Newfie grins from ear to ear. "Thanks be to Jesus," he says. "I thought I'd have to stay here for another week."

A Newfie and a Torontonian are stranded at sea. They managed to save a few supplies and have stored them in one end of the small dingy that they're floating in. The Newfie is rummaging through the supplies and finds an old lamp. He has no idea what they can use the lamp for, but the Torontonian tells him it might contain a genie. Crossing his fingers, the Newfie rubs the lamp and, to their surprise, a genie appears. He offers the men one wish between them. The Newfie says, "I wish the sea was made of rum." Poof! The sea turns to rum, and the genie disappears.

The Torontonian turns to look at the Newfie and says, "Now look what you've done. We're gonna have to piss in the boat from now on!"

Two Newfies walk out of a bar in Ontario. They get into an argument over who should drive. The first Newfie says, "Look, buddy, you only drank six beers and I had eight beers and two shots. You got to drive."

The second Newfie says, "You're cracked. I might have only had six beers, but I had three Lambs and Cokes, too."

The two Newfies go back and forth for several minutes before the first Newfie grabs the keys out of his buddy's hand and says, "Gimme dem, I'll drive."

So the Newfie starts driving and swerving all over the road. First they swerve left, and then they swerve right.

The second Newfie looks at the first and says, "By God, me son, what is you up to tonight?"

The first Newfie says, "Jumpin' dyin', I'm just staying away from dose trees!"

The second Newfie looks over and says, "By the Jesus! That there is your air freshener."

En route to Alberta, an airplane leaves St. John's airport and reaches its cruising altitude. The captain comes on over the intercom. "Welcome to Flight 619 from St. John's to Edmonton. We have reached our cruising altitude and see nothing but blue skies ahead. Please sit back and enjoy the ser–...Oh my God...!"

The intercom goes silent as the plane dips erratically and the passengers scream.

The plane eventually levels out, and after a few tense minutes, the captain speaks again. "I'm sorry if I scared you, ladies and gentlemen. The flight attendant brought me a cup of coffee and spilled it in my lap. You should see the front of my pants," the pilot laughs.

A Newfie passenger in the back of the plane yells, "Dat's nuttin'. You should see the arse of mine!"

A Newfie living in Calgary wakes up one morning and decides he is going to do something he has never done before. After looking through the YellowPages, he decides to go skydiving. He finds an instructor and starts taking lessons. The instructor explains to the Newfie that he has to jump out of the plane, count to 10 and give his ripcord a hard yank. The instructor also says he will jump out behind the Newfie, and they will go down together. The Newfie nods to the instructor that he's ready. They climb into the plane and are off.

It gets close jumping time, so the instructor reminds the Newfie to jump, count to 10 and pull the ripcord. The instructor tells the Newfie not to worry and that he will be right behind him. The Newfie proceeds to jump from the plane and after counting to 10, pulls the ripcord. The instructor follows the Newfie, but when he pulls his ripcord, nothing happens. The instructor sails past the Newfie, headed for the ground.

The Newfie, having none of that, undoes the straps on his parachute and yells at the instructor, "All right den, buddy, it's a race!"

John and Frank are working at a job site in Fort McMurray. Both of them are tired from the night before, so John turns to Frank and says, "Frankie, my boy, I bet you $100 I can get the rest of the day off."

Frank smiles and says, "You're full of shit, but let's see you do it."

John walks over to the foreman, stands straight as a poker and whispers, "I'm a burnt-out light bulb." He doesn't move a muscle or say another word.

The foreman eyes him strangely and says, "There's something wrong with you Newfies; get out of here and take the rest of the day off."

John winks at Frank and leaves. When Frank follows, close on his heels, the foreman yells, "Where do you think you're going?"

Frank says calmly, "Well, sir, ya don't expect me to work in the dark, do ya?"

A man from Edmonton goes to see a psychiatrist and complains, "Doctor, I'm not doing very well. Every night I lie in bed and can't fall asleep. I know someone is under my bed waiting to get me."

The psychiatrist listens to the man and says, "I can certainly help you with that. Set up appointments for three times a week, and in under a year, your fears will be gone."

The man quickly asks, "How much do you charge?"

"Eighty dollars per visit," the doctor answers.

The man says, "I'll think about it and decide later."

Six months pass, and the doctor sees the man on the street and asks him why he didn't set up another appointment.

The man says, "Well, you were going to charge me too much money, and then I ran into a Newfie friend of mine, and he cured me in one day."

The doctor is amazed and replies, "One day, that's incredible! How did he cure you in one day?"

The man smiles and says, "He told me to cut the legs off my bed. Now there can't be anyone under there."

A Newfie is working at a construction site in Toronto. One day he shows up for work at noon. His boss, disgusted at the Newfie's late arrival, says, "You should have been here at eight o'clock this morning."

The Newfie asks, "Why, what happened?"

A Newfie goes to a job interview for a logging company in Ontario, and passes the HR rep his application. On the application, the Newfie has written that he left his old workplace because of sickness. The HR rep knows the job the Newfie is applying for is physically demanding, so he needs to know if the Newfie is able to perform any and all tasks he might be given. The HR rep asks the Newfie to explain further the nature of his sickness and why it caused him to leave his old job.

The Newfie looks at the HR rep and says, "Well, b'y, me old boss got sick of me."

Three contractors are bidding on a contract to fix a fence at the parliament buildings in Ottawa. One contractor is from Alberta, one is from Newfoundland and the other is from Quebec. The three contractors meet a government official onsite to inspect the broken fence.

The contractor from Alberta measures the fence, pulls out his laptop and enters the numbers into it. After a few minutes, he comes back with a bid: $900 ($400 for his men, $400 for materials and $100 profit).

The contractor from Newfoundland steps up, measures the fence, pulls out a notepad and does his figuring by hand. His bid: $700 ($300 for his men, $300 for materials and $100 profit).

The contractor from Quebec doesn't move from where he's standing. He doesn't measure or calculate any numbers. After a few minutes of not doing anything, he whispers his bid to the government official: $2700. The government official is taken aback. He whispers to the Quebecer, "Where did you come up with that figure? You didn't measure anything."

The contractor whispers back, "$1000 for me, $1000 for you and we hire the Newfie to fix the fence."

"Done deal!" says the government official.

Letters from Fort McMurray

MAY 30—I just pitched in Fort McMurray. This is the place for me. The sun shines all the time. There is lots of trouting and quading. Everyone tells me to watch out for the bugs, but I haven't seen any yet. It's like God picked up Newfoundland and found her a sunny place in heaven. I love it here!

JUNE 14—I got a job out at the plants, and everything is going great. The pay is good. There's lots of other Newfies around. Everyone likes to spend time outdoors. Last week we went quading and saw three deer and some crazy bugs. One bit me, but 'twas nuthin'. This is an outdoorsman's paradise.

JUNE 30—Went on a trouting trip. I got bit by three more bugs. One of them bites won't heal. Going to the doctor tomorrow. All is still well.

JULY 10—The bug bite is still not healed, and the doctor can't figure out what to do with it. He wants me to go back into the woods and find a bug like it. I'm concerned about my arm, but other than that 'tis goin' good.

JULY 15—I managed to find a bug like the one that bit me. He was hard to catch, but I tracked him down. At one point, the bugger chased me for three hours, but I wrestled him to the ground. On the way out I got two more bites and one started to fester last night. Back to the doctor in the morning. I think the bugs are following me truck.

JULY 20—The doctor can't figure out what the name of the bug is. My arm has turned purple, and the doctor thinks it might be infected. The bug has been sent out to some lab in Edmonton. I t'inks the bugs hate me.

JULY 25—Ended up in the hospital. The bug bite is worse today. Some idiot left the door open, and I got bit on the leg. That one looks just as bad as the others, but the ones on me arms have joined together, and the doctor now only counts them as one bite.

JULY 30—The lab sent the bug back and asked if they could have a live one. I sent me buddies out to find one, and they got bit and had to shoot the bug that bit them. No luck on the live bug. The lab got mad and says there's nothing they can do. Fort McMurray ain't the funnest place right now.

AUGUST 10—I lost all feeling in my arm. The bites that joined together caused me arm to swell somethin' fierce. My leg still hurts somethin' terrible. No one can come see me 'cause I'm not allowed any visitors. Thanks for the molasses jimmies you sent. The nurses liked them a lot.

AUGUST 19—I got out of the hospital today. I can't get no one sick now, but I can't have no children, either. The doctor told me to stay away from bugs, but they is everywhere. They follow you and knock on your window at night. I can't travel for a while yet. McMurray is the worst place on Earth.

SEPTEMBER 2—It started to cool down today. The bugs disappeared, thanks be to Jesus. I couldn't stand another day inside. I went for a walk and broke my leg. No more bugs, but I have crutches. I booked my plane ticket for next week.

SEPTEMBER 7—Had a going away party at the Newfie Club. Got drunk. Fell down. Broke other leg. Hate Fort McMurray, can't wait to get back to The Rock.

Garge and Fred get laid off from the same Ontario factory. They both get up the next morning and off they go to the EI office to get their employment insurance set up. Garge sits down in front of the clerk and tells her he used to make sweaters. Without another word, the clerk tells him that he'll get $300 every week. Garge is pretty happy with that and leaves the office.

Fred walks in, sits in front of the same clerk and announces he was a diesel fitter. The clerk is surprised that a diesel fitter worked at a sweater factory, but she informs Fred that he'll get $600 every week. He is happy enough with that and walks out. Proud as a peacock, he tells Garge what he'll be getting.

Hearing the news, Garge gets mad and storms into the clerk's office, "Listen 'ere, missus. How come Fred gets more than me? We worked side-by-side at the same place."

The clerk explains that Fred is a diesel fitter, and that is worth more EI than a sweater-maker.

Garge laughs, "Diesel fitter...yeah. I makes the sweaters and Fred tries 'em on and if they're good he says, 'Dees 'il fit her.'"

MAINLANDER: "Why do divers fall backward out of a boat?"

NEWFIE: "Because if they fall forward, they are still in the damn boat."

A Newfie is walking down the street in Calgary wearing a glove on his right hand, but his left hand is bare. Everyone who walks past ends up staring at the Newfie. Someone finally has the nerve to ask what's up with the one glove.

The Newfie looks around and says, "Well, 'tis like dis, b'y. Ya never know'd what the weather will be—on one 'and it might be sunny and warm, but on the other 'and it might be windy and cold."

Boyd, from Arnold's Cove, goes to the fanciest doctor he can find in Montreal. He complains extensively that every place he touches hurts like nuttin' else he ever felt. The doctor takes X-rays, runs blood work and sends Boyd for more tests, but he doesn't find anything amiss. Boyd appears to be in perfect health.

Boyd stands up and pokes himself in the arm, the leg and the chest and says, "Doc, der got to be somethin' the matter. I touches here; it hurts. I touches here; it hurts. Anywhere I touches, it hurts."

The doctor finally figures out the problem. He grabs Boyd's finger and Boyd nearly hits the ceiling. It hurts so bad Boyd screams, "Lard Jesus, doc! What you do that for?"

The doctor replies, "Sir, I think it's fairly obvious what is wrong. Your finger is broken and it requires a cast."

Harv is just about to leave Newfoundland and drive to Alberta when he looks at his father and says, "Fadder, b'y, I knows it sounds silly, but I'm gonna miss the island so much. I'm afraid I'll be homesick."

Harv's father looks at him and says, "Harv, me son, here's what you do: strap dat old dory to yer truck. Den when you misses home, go for a little row."

Harv thinks his father's idea is a bit daft, but he goes along with the suggestion. He leaves and is fine all through the Maritimes, only stops for gas and smokes in Quebec and the Great Lakes don't make him miss home. But when Harv hits Manitoba, he sees wheat fields for miles and the waving of the grass reminds him of the sea.

So just like his father said, Harv pulls over and drags the dory from his truck. He manages to get it out in the middle of a field where he is surrounded by wheat. Harv rows for a while and thinks about Newfoundland.

Q: What do you call someone standing on the side of the road in Quebec?

A: A Newfie who ran out of gas on his way to Alberta.

He's just getting ready to pull the dory back to his truck when a small car pulls up, and the driver jumps out and starts yelling and shaking his fists.

Harv hears him cry out, "My God, yer de one who makes Newfies look stupid, and my sonny b'y, if I could swim I'd be out der just like dat to sink yer boat!"

Bill and John, two Newfies from Fortune, are driving to Fort McMurray when they pass a truck loaded down with sod.

Bill turns to John and says, "Will ya look at dat? B'y, when I gets all that money from them oil sands and builds a house, I'm gonna send me grass out to get cut, too."

A Newfie walks into The Big Slice on Yonge Street in Toronto and asks to buy a whole pizza. The clerk asks if he wants it cut into 6 or 12 slices.

The Newfie looks up and replies, "Six, b'y. Pretty sure I can't eat 12."

A Newfie who has been living on the mainland for several years goes to visit friends of his on their farm in rural Ontario. When he's leaving, they offer him some cucumbers. The cucumbers are straight from their garden, he is told. The Newfie politely declines the offer, telling his friends he doesn't really like cucumbers. The friends look surprised and comment that he likes pickles.

The Newfie responds, "Pickles? What the hell do they have to do with cucumbers?"

A Newfie who is living in Toronto goes to a travel agent to book his trip back home. The travel agent asks him where he is headed. The Newfie tells her he needs a ticket to St. John's, and while she is checking available flights, he starts listing other demands for his trip.

"Okay," the Newfie says, "I need one bag to go from here to Calgary, and then to Vancouver and then to St. John's. And I need the other bag to go from here to Ottawa, then to Edmonton, then to St. John's."

The travel agent looks at him and says, "Sir, that isn't possible. Your suitcases must be on the same flight as you. There is no way we can send them to different places while you travel direct to St. John's."

The Newfie replies calmly, "Well, I don't know what the problem is. The last time I went home, that's where my bags went before I got them."

A sailor is making an international call from England to Newfoundland. He has to speak to the operator to get the call completed. The operator asks him where he is calling.

"Fartune," the sailor says.

The operator asks, "Pardon, sir?"

He says, "Get I Fartune."

The operator asks the sailor once more to repeat where he wants to call.

The sailor gets upset at the operator's lack of understanding and yells, "Listen here, missus! I says Fartune—F-A-R-T-U-N-E."

A Newfie walks into a bar on the top floor of a hotel in Vancouver. He pulls up a stool and takes a seat beside two strangers. After more than a few beers, the first stranger goes over to the window and jumps out. The Newfie is shocked to see him walk through the elevator a few minutes later without so much as a scratch.

The Newfie looks at the stranger and says, "My God, buddy, how'd ya pull dat off?"

Q: Did you hear about the war between Newfoundland and Nova Scotia?

A: The Newfies were throwing hand grenades at Nova Scotia, and the Nova Scotians were pulling the pins and throwing them back.

The stranger replies, "Oh, it's easy. Just jump and spread your wings."

The Newfie leaps up, runs over to the window and throws himself out. He doesn't come back to the bar.

The second stranger looks up from his beer and says, "Superman, you are one mean drunk!"

A Newfie walks into a big Vancouver hotel. He's carrying a suitcase and walking arm-in-arm with his wife. A hotel attendant approaches the Newfie and says, "Carry your bag, sir?"

The Newfie stops, thinks for a moment and smiles at the attendant, "Nah, she can walk herself."

A Newfie, an Albertan and a Frenchman are set to go into space for three months. Just as they are getting ready to board the space shuttle, they are asked what one luxury item they want to take with them.

The Frenchman thinks about it and says, "Sir, I must request wine at every meal." Cases of his favourite wine are loaded onto the space shuttle.

The Albertan says, "Well, I'd like steak every day." Steaks are loaded into the cargo bay of the shuttle.

The Newfie stops and looks at everyone, "Well, I gots to have my smokes and there is no way 'round that." Cartons of his favourite smokes are loaded onto the space shuttle.

After three months in space the astronauts finally come home. As they step off the shuttle, a reporter asks them about their trip.

The Frenchman comments, "The wine was magnificent. It made me feel quite at home."

The Albertan says, "Yee-haw! The steak was perfect."

The Newfie lifts a shaking hand and shouts, "Got a light?"

A Newfie tries to walk into the hottest nightclub in Kingston, Ontario. He gets stopped at the door by one of the biggest bouncers he has ever seen. The bouncer looks at him and says, "Sorry, friend, you need a tie for this place. You can't come in without one."

The Newfie goes back to his car and rummages around, but there isn't anything inside that remotely resembles a tie. He really wants to get into the nightclub, but he doesn't want to drive home to find a tie, either.

Finally, in desperation, he looks in the trunk and spies his jumper cables. He wraps them around his neck, ties a nice knot and lets the ends dangle free. Proud as a new father, he heads back to the nightclub.

He stands in line and waits his turn. When the bouncer calls him forward, the Newfie puffs up his chest and stands in front of the bouncer, large as life.

The bouncer looks at him strangely and after a few minutes says, "Well, I guess you can come in. But don't you dare try and start anything!"

Q: How did the Toronto car salesman fit seven Newfies in a Smart Car?

A: He told them it was headed to Fort McMurray.

Q: How did the Fort McMurray car salesman fit nine Newfies in a Smart Car?

A: He told them it was headed back to Newfoundland.

A Newfie is on a business trip to New York City and walks into the most expensive lingerie store he can find. As a Valentine's Day present to himself, he wants to buy his wife the sheerest lingerie they have in the store.

The woman behind the counter goes and gets an outfit.

"This is $200," she says.

"I wants one dat's more see-through than dat there," the Newfie says.

The sales lady goes in back and returns with another piece of lingerie.

"This one is $350," she says.

"Come on now, missus, you must have somet'ing even better than dat," the Newfie replies. Once again she goes away and returns, holding up a negligee that you can barely see.

She presents the garment to the Newfie and says, "This one is the sheerest we have. It's $500."

"I'll take dat one!" the Newfie exclaims. He returns home to his wife and shows it to her. He asks her to model it for him.

The Newfie's wife goes upstairs, opens the box and thinks, "My God, dis t'ing is so see-through dat the fool won't even notice if I got it on. I can send dis back for a refund and buy somethin' dat I wants."

Coming out wearing nothing at all, the Newfie's wife strikes a model pose at the top of the stairs.

"So, what do you t'ink about dis?" she asks.

The Newfie gets angry and replies, "Holy Moses! You'd t'ink for $500 dey could have ironed the damn t'ing!"

Two Newfies are sitting front and centre at the bar in the Newfie Club in Fort McMurray.

One says to the other, "Where is you from, me son?"

The man replies, "My God, sure I'm from Newfoundland."

The first Newfie gets excited and says, "Jesus, b'y, I'm from Newfoundland, too! Let me buy you a drink, my friend."

The bartender brings each of them a fresh pint, and they continue talking.

> Q: How did the Newfie tell the mainlander to kill a fish?
>
> A: Drown it.

The first Newfie asks where the other man grew up.

The other Newfie responds, "I grew up in Gander, b'y."

The first Newfie gets excited and says, "Lard Jeezus, I was born in Gander, too!" He buys another round of pints.

The first Newfie asks one more question, "Where did you go to school at?"

The second Newfie explains, "B'y, the last school I went to was Gander Collegiate."

This piece of news excites the first Newfie so much that he jumps off the stool and calls out, "By God, I went to Gander Collegiate, too! Did you happen to know me brother, Jim Smith?"

While listening to the conversation going on in front of him, the bartender answers the phone. He nods his head and answers the caller's question, saying, "Oh nuthin' much is goin' on here. The Smith twins are drunk again, though."

A gorgeous blonde woman decides she's going to commit suicide by throwing herself off the pier in North Sydney. She stands looking down at the water when a handsome young Newfie walks up to her and asks what she's doing. The woman explains what's going on, and the gallant Newfie tries to stop her.

"Look here, missus," he says. "I don't got no idea what's going on in yer life, but you gots lots to live for. I'm sailing to England tomorrow, and I can stow you away on the ship for the entire trip." He slips his arm around her waist and whispers in her ear, "I'll keep you happy, and you can keep me happy. Okay, my dear?"

The blonde decides right then and there that a trip to England is the best thing that can ever happen to her.

Later that night, the Newfie dresses her in a funny uniform and hides her in a lifeboat. Every night for three weeks, the Newfie brings her food and they have passionate sex until dawn.

During routine maintenance of the lifeboats, the blonde is discovered and brought before the captain. "What were you doing inside that lifeboat?" the captain asks.

"I made a deal with one of the sailors. He's taking me to England," the blonde says as she starts to cry.

The captain looks at her and says, "My dear, you're on the ferry to Newfoundland."

How to Tell if Someone Is a Bayman Living on the Mainland

They go to a Newfie club, which always features a bar.

They speak with an accent that mainlanders can't understand, and they don't care if it's understandable or not.

They congregate in kitchens where drinking, playing music and dancing are sure to occur.

They always talk about going "home" and by that they always mean Newfoundland.

They are handy and can fix almost anything. Well, they will try to fix almost anything.

There are two teams of telephone pole installers working along the Labrador/Quebec border. One team is made up of mainlanders, and the other team is made up entirely of Newfies. The project manager walks up to the teams and tells them that because of budget cuts, they can only afford to keep one crew on staff. To decide which group gets to stay, the teams decide to have a contest. The team that can erect the most poles in three days gets to stay on the job.

At the end of the first day, both teams report how many poles they have installed. The mainlanders say they have installed 25 poles, while the Newfies report they have only installed 15.

By the end of the second day, the mainlanders have installed another 15, but the Newfies have only managed 10.

Q: How did the Newfie move to Alberta and not have to change his address?

A: He took the numbers on his house with him.

At the end of the third and last day of the contest, the mainlanders have installed a total of 55 poles, while the poor old Newfies have only installed a total of 40.

The project manager informs the teams that the mainlanders have won, and they will be the group that gets to keep working.

The Newfies get angry at the news and complain, "B'y, that's not fair a'toll. Them fellers is only installin' the poles halfway."

Sally, a young Newfie woman, is sent to work at Tim Hortons in Afghanistan for six months. Her job is to serve coffee to the members of the Canadian Forces stationed there. She really enjoys the job and writes to her boyfriend every day, telling him about the differences between Afghanistan and home.

After about three months, she receives a "Dear John" letter from her boyfriend. He says that a long-distance relationship isn't for him. He thought he could handle her being gone for six months, but he can't. In the letter, he even admits he has already cheated on her. At the end, he requests that she send back the picture he gave her before she left.

Sally is devastated at the news. She gets angry and devises a plan to get back at her so-called boy-friend. She asks everyone around her to donate a picture to her cause. Once they hear the story, they are more than happy to give her pictures.

Sally gathers up the pictures and writes the fol-lowing note to her boyfriend:

Dear Buddy,

I'm really sorry, but I can't quite remember what you looks like. Please take your picture from the pile that I put in with this note and send the rest of the pictures back to me.

Thanks,

Sally

A Newfie is sitting in a pub in Boston, and he keeps looking at his watch every few minutes.

A woman sitting two stools away notices he keeps looking at the time and asks, "Excuse me, is your date for the evening running a little late?"

The Newfie shakes his head and tries to explain what's going on. "See, on me arm I've got the latest and greatest watch ever invented, and I'm testing it out to make sure it works."

Intrigued, the woman asks, "What's so great about that particular watch?"

The Newfie explains, "It uses special brainwaves to talk to me. It tells me things that no one could ever know. I bought it from a really expensive store in Toronto. They told me it was a one-of-a-kind experimental watch."

The woman moves to sit beside the Newfie and says suggestively, "Well, then, what is your watch telling you right now?"

The Newfie bravely looks her up and down and replies, "My watch is telling me that right now you aren't wearing any underwear."

The woman winks at the Newfie and says, "I'm sorry, but your watch is wrong. I can guarantee that I'm wearing a red silk thong."

The Newfie grins at the woman and says slyly, "Damn thing is running fast. Can I buy you a drink?"

Someone told an Ontarian that English is some-day going to be the most popular language in the world. The Ontarian asked who is going to tell Newfoundland.

Two Newfies are strolling down the street in Toronto. They spot a sign in a store window that reads, "Suits $5 each, shirts $2 each, trousers $2.50 per pair."

The first Newfie says, "Look at dat, me son! We could buy a whole whack of dees clothes, send 'em to St. John's, get Barry to sell 'em and make a ton of money. We is gonna be rich!"

His friend agrees to the plan. But just to be sure they get the deal of a lifetime, the first Newfie lays down some rules. "Now den, when we goes in der, you be quiet. You let me do the talking. Dees mainlanders is a shifty lot. If'n dey gets wind that we is from Newfoundland dey might not want to sell us the stuff. I'll talk right fancy, like I'm from Ontario, and dey won't sure even know the difference."

The Newfies walk into the store, and the first Newfie stands at the counter and starts to talk using his best mainlander accent. He says, "Excuse me, sir, I'll take 50 suits at $5 each, 100 shirts at $2 each and 50 pairs of trousers at $2.50 each. My friend here will just pull our automobile around the back."

The owner of the shop stops him. "You boys wouldn't by any chance happen to be from Newfoundland, would you?"

"Well…yeah," says the first Newfie, scratching his head. "B'y, how'd you manage to figure us out?"

The owner rolls his eyes and replies, "Because you're at the dry cleaners."

Garge is watching his Toronto neighbour try and build a patio. He watches the neighbour unload what looks like a ton of patio bricks. The neighbour tries to lay them out in a pattern, and after all his work, stacks them beside the house.

The next day Garge watches his neighbour clear some more space, lay out the bricks, move them around a lot and then stack them up beside the house.

The day after that, a truck arrives with a load of sand. Garge watches his neighbour spread out the sand, arrange the bricks, move them around for a few hours and then stack them up beside the house again.

After watching this for several days, Garge leans over the fence and says, "Buddy, do I have to watch you pack up that patio every single night?"

Conclusion

And that's it. You've learned how to talk like a Newfie, you've read the jokes we tell about ourselves and about everyone else and, along the way, I hope you managed a chuckle or two.

Newfies like to laugh, and we like to make others laugh, even if it's at our own expense. But all jokes aside, Dildo was a great place to grow up, and Newfoundland is still one of the best places to call home. As the saying goes:

> *Don't cry too hard 'cause you weren't born in Newfoundland, me son. If you is good enough, you'll end up here when you dies.*

Natasha White

Born in St. John's, Newfoundland, Natasha White was raised in Dildo, where she undoubtedly developed her witty sense of humour. She completed high school in Newfoundland and moved to Alberta, where she makes a living through her writing. She has also entered and won a short fiction contest for a Newfoundland magazine. Now an Albertan, she bundles up against the chilly prairie winters and longs for the Atlantic Ocean.

Illustrator

Roger Garcia is a self-taught artist with some formal training who specializes in cartooning and illustration. He is an immigrant from El Salvador, and during the last few years, his work has been primarily cartoons and editorial illustrations in pen and ink. Recently he has started painting once more, focusing on simplifying the human form, using a bright minimal palette and as few elements as possible. His work can be seen in newspapers, magazines and promo material and on www.rogergarcia.ca.